SATURDAY PIZZAS

from the Ballymaloe Cookery School

SATURDAY PIZZAS

from the Ballymaloe Cookery School

The essential guide to making pizza at home,
from perfect classics to inspired gourmet toppings

PHILIP DENNHARDT + KRISTIN JENSEN

photography by Mowie Kay

RYLAND PETERS & SMALL
LONDON • NEW YORK

Dedication

For DMO – we laughed and cried together

Recipe writer and developer Kristin Jensen

Senior Designer Barbara Zuñiga
Editor Alice Sambrook
Text Editors Jane Bamforth and Lesley Malkin
Head of Production Patricia Harrington
Editorial Director Julia Charles
Art Director Leslie Harrington
Publisher Cindy Richards

Food Stylists Emily Kidd and Maud Eden
Prop Stylist Jo Harris
Indexer Hilary Bird

First published in 2017 by
Ryland Peters & Small
20–21 Jockey's Fields
London WC1R 4BW
and
341 E 116th Street
New York, 10029

www.rylandpeters.com

10 9 8 7 6 5 4 3 2 1

Text copyright © Philip Dennhardt 2017
Design and commissioned photography copyright © Ryland
Peters & Small 2017. Image on page 10 supplied courtesy of
The Ballymaloe Cookery School © Tim Allen.

ISBN: 978-1-84975-882-6

A CIP record for this book is available from the British Library.
US Library of Congress CIP data has been applied for.

Printed in China

Notes
- Both metric and imperial (plus US cup measurements)
  are included in this book, but it is important to work
  with one set of measurements only and not alternate
  between the two within a recipe. However, the
  authors recommend that all ingredients are weighed
  rather than measured in cups where possible (for
  more detail, see pages 15 and 23).
- Oven temperatures given are for fan-assisted ovens.
- One 7 g ($\frac{1}{4}$ oz) sachet of fast action dried yeast is
  equivalent to $2\frac{1}{4}$ teaspoons.
- All eggs are UK large/US extra-large.

CONTENTS

FOREWORD by Darina Allen, Ballymaloe Cookery School

It's such a joy for me to write a foreword to this book for many reasons, not least because Philip, who is married to my youngest daughter Emily, has breathed new life into the wood-fired oven that I bought back in the 1980s. There is a special magic to cooking in a wood-burning oven. It takes considerable skill to build a fire, judge the heat and feed extra logs of dry timber to keep the embers glowing at the correct temperature to cook the food to perfection. It needs to be super-hot to cook a thin-crust pizza in three minutes or less, so that it has a crisp base, a bubbly crust and a meltingly flavourful topping.

The highly esteemed authors Marcella and Victor Hazan introduced me to this kind of cooking on my first trip to Emilia-Romagna in northern Italy. I was intrigued by the idea of having an outdoor bread oven in a vineyard and longed to have one at the Ballymaloe Cookery School. After a lot of research, which took me from the west coast of California to the River Café in London and eventually, on the recommendation of American chef Alice Waters, back to the source in Italy, we bought a kit from Valoriani, a company that is renowned for the quality of its ovens.

In 2007 Philip came to us with an idea for a pop-up pizzeria on Saturdays and wondered whether we would be happy for him to experiment in the wood-fired oven in the Garden Café at the school. We're always excited by a new venture, so of course we said yes.

Philip hankered after those delicious pizzas he had tasted in California and was excited about incorporating the fresh organic produce from our farm and gardens with fish and shellfish from the nearby fishing village at Ballycotton. He made a pilgrimage to Italy and tasted pizzas from Rome to Naples. Back home, he experimented with flours and doughs until he was happy with the crust. The result delighted us all and soon Saturday Pizzas had a cult following. There was always a Margherita and pepperoni, but also a new vegetarian and non-vegetarian pizza, reflecting the seasons. Philip is meticulous about his research, recording each week's specials and tweaking the recipes. He is always creative and inspired by the fresh ingredients, artisan produce and foraged foods around us, and every Saturday we look forward to the specials.

One day Philip told me that he would love to write a pizza cookbook and the next thing I know, he asked me to write the foreword. Now here it is, a beautifully written book that will inspire even those who have never made a pizza before to have a go. And you don't need to own a wood-burning oven – you can get excellent results in a conventional oven. As I read through Philip's mouth-watering recipes, I couldn't help thinking how far pizza has come since I was at hotel and catering college in Dublin in the early 1960s. Pizza was a very precise thing: a base slathered with a concentrated tomato sauce, topped with a lattice of anchovy fillets with a black olive in the centre of every diamond. It never occurred to me to experiment with alternative toppings until I tasted Wolfgang Puck's beautiful thin-crust pizza topped with shrimp, fresh tomato and basil leaves at a reception in Los Angeles in the mid-1980s. It was a eureka moment.

The fun continues every week with Philip's carefully chosen combinations. Some are traditional, but there are some unorthodox concoctions too, such as apple and black pudding, or braised beef with BBQ sauce and pickled red onions, perhaps finished with a drizzle of homemade aioli, hoisin sauce, gremolata or tapenade and served with a salad of organic leaves with edible flowers on top.

When you start making your own pizza, there's no end to the fun. Once you have made the dough, there are many more options than just pizza. You can make calzone, sfincione, stromboli, panzerotti, piadina, sgabei ... the list goes on. I hope you will be inspired by Philip to release your inner pizzaiolo.

INTRODUCTION
How it all began: From master butcher to Berkeley to Ballymaloe

I was the fourth generation of my family to train as a master butcher in Germany, so I never dreamed that one day I'd end up making pizza in Ireland. When I was 18 I decided to do the three-year apprenticeship to see what might come of it, even though I already knew it wasn't what I wanted to do with my life. Out of 3,000 students, I finished with the highest marks, but I still felt that it was time to do something different. I was thinking of studying economics, but when my former boss heard about my plan, he said, 'Philip, don't do it. There's a job in New York, it's a once-in-a-lifetime opportunity.' He was right. When would I ever get the chance to live and work in New York again? So I took it.

One day I was standing on 42nd Street waiting for a friend when I felt a tap on my shoulder. I turned around and standing there was an Irish girl from work. To cut a long story short, when the job ended, I moved back to Ireland with her. It turned out that the Irish girl I'd fallen in love with was the daughter of Darina Allen, founder of the world-famous Ballymaloe Cookery School.

Darina gave me a job at the school in 2005, where I learned everything from making compost to cooking a three-course meal, from milking cows to harvesting seaweed. I then started running a cupcake business at the local farmers' market with Darina. We have a saying in Germany: 'craft has a golden foundation'. My master butcher qualification and everything I had learned and done at the cookery school stood me in good stead, but I still didn't really know what I wanted to do. So in 2007 I took a break from the school and spent a few months working in one of the most iconic restaurants in America, Chez Panisse in Berkeley, California.

Right across the street from Chez Panisse is a place called the Cheese Board Collective. It's a worker-owned co-operative where you can buy delicious cheese from all over the world as well as homemade bread, pastries and pizza. I passed the shop several times every day and whenever I walked by, I'd see dozens of people queuing up to buy pizza. What was going on? Curiosity got the better of me and I had to see for myself.

There is only one type of pizza every day and it's always vegetarian. There's a wine of the day and a salad and payment is by cash or cheque. That's it. Simple. After that first visit to the Cheese Board, I was buzzing with ideas. I immediately realized that this was how I could do something new at the cookery school. It would be a win-win for everyone. But how could I create something like that myself? And then I had my eureka moment: there is a wood-burning oven in the Garden Café at the Ballymaloe Cookery School with a kitchen and a big dining room, but it wasn't being used at the weekends. It would literally take a single spark to create a pizzeria.

As soon as I got back to Ireland, I ran the idea by Darina. She was completely supportive of my vision and said I should go for it. The cookery school only operated from Monday to Friday, so Saturday Pizzas was born.

We fired up the oven and served our first pizza in May 2008. It was a hit from the start. A steady stream of people would come every week, sometimes with queues out the door. It began as a pop-up that closed for the winter, but it quickly became a year-round institution.

Before Saturday Pizzas started, access to the cookery school was limited as the only way you could visit was to take a course or sit in on a demo. One of the great things about Saturday Pizzas is that it has opened the door for people to visit the school, stroll around the gardens and farm shop and have an inexpensive dinner too.

The wood-burning oven at Ballymaloe

My first encounter with a wood-burning oven was in Italy in the 1980s and later at Alice Waters's Chez Panisse restaurant in Berkeley, California, where the most irresistible food was emerging from it. I had loved the flavour of the food since tasting Wolfgang Puck's bubbly thin crust pizza in Los Angeles a few years previously and so when we opened the Garden Café at the school in the summer of 1998, I decided I wanted a wood-fired oven of my own. So I went to California on a research trip.

My journey took me to Mendocino County where, behind the community centre in a small town called Elk, we found a clay adobe oven large enough to roast a pig. I soon discovered that the man behind many of the great ovens that I saw was an oven-builder from New Zealand, called Alan Scott, who had since returned home to his native country. When I arrived at Chez Panisse, Alice told me all about the vagaries of their wood-burning oven as there had been some teething problems, and suggested I forget about trying to have one built, romantic as that was; better to go to the Italians, who have been making wood-burning ovens for centuries, and buy a kit. She found me the name of a brilliantly efficient Italian company and, much to my amazement, I had the oven within six weeks. The company gave brilliant instructions for installation, in English, and I also took my builder over to see the River Café's oven in Hammersmith to observe it in operation. Ruth Rogers and the late Rose Gray said it was instrumental in their cooking and they used it every day – so it was a good place to go to see how this type of oven could work.

In 1998 we found a young chef, Stevie O'Brien Gleeson, who had been working with a wood oven in Tosca, a pizzeria in Suffolk Street in Dublin. Stevie spent the summer season with us in the Garden Café and taught us how to work with fire. People came from far and wide for the pizza – the café was open seven days a week and the students loved it too. That year, Stevie concentrated on pizza, but the following year my son, Isaac, became more adventurous – he made a delicious roast tomato soup and we also used the oven to roast fish, meat and vegetables.

In May 2008, 10 years after its installation, our son-in-law, Philip Dennhardt, decided to do a 'pop-up' pizzeria from 12.30–4pm every Saturday in the Garden Café (the school is usually closed on a Saturday so the dining room is open to the public). It has proved so popular that Saturday Pizzas are now an institution – there's cool music and a fun atmosphere plus the 12-week students get the opportunity to learn how it all works, on a rota basis, and to cook with fire – the half-day pizza, calzone, panzerotti, piadina and sfinciuni demonstration is an integral part of the course.

Wood-burning ovens are now quite widespread – popular in many restaurants and not just pizzerias. You'll often see mobile ones at farmers' markets and festivals and many people build small versions in their gardens. Philip Dennhardt gives a pizza workshop using the wood-burning oven at the Ballymaloe Cookery School several times a year and Simon Mould, who now runs the 'Volcano Pizza' stand at the Midleton Farmers' Market, is an old student of his. The regulators, who were wary of this trend at the outset, have become more accepting of it and realize that cooking in wood-burning ovens is a time-honoured tradition, which adds immeasurably to the flavour of food.

From *30 Years at Ballymaloe* by Darina Allen

A typical day at Saturday Pizzas

I try to keep things as simple as possible at the pizzeria. First, every Friday morning, we make the pizza dough so that it can ferment for about 36 hours, which produces a beautiful pizza crust. We have a stroll through the cookery school's organic gardens and glasshouses to see what ingredients are ready to be harvested. We use fresh, local and organic ingredients as much as possible, which means our pizza toppings reflect the seasons too. You'll see wild garlic or nettles being used on our pizzas in the spring, courgettes/zucchini and homegrown sweetcorn in the summer as well as fresh tomatoes, peppers and aubergines/eggplant from the glasshouses, then pumpkin and Tuscan kale in the autumn and roasted root vegetables in the winter. Sometimes we even use foraged ingredients, such as sea kale or chanterelle mushrooms. Once we've seen what we have in the gardens, we also check what needs to be used up from the cookery school, which could be extra salad leaves or half a wheel of cheese or even a few lobsters. Needless to say, it's an incredible luxury to be able to play around and cook with these kinds of ingredients.

All the staff arrive at 11am. I have a great team and I couldn't run the pizzeria without them, so the first thing I do is thank everyone for coming. I like to think of this as creating a cycle of gratitude – I thank my staff from the heart, which is then reflected in how they treat our customers, because I'm also grateful for each and every person who walks through our door. I end every week's staff meeting by reminding them to treat everyone like a VIP.

We light the wood-burning oven on Saturday morning and make sure there is enough wood for a day's baking (we need two or three wheelbarrows full of wood to see us through the afternoon), then we organize the kitchen and get all the ingredients for the pizzas ready. Because we operate on such a small scale we prep a lot of ingredients by hand, be it grating Parmesan on a big box grater or painstakingly peeling garlic cloves.

The Margherita and pepperoni pizzas are our flagships, so we can practically do the prep for those blindfolded. More thought and effort go into the special pizzas, which change every week. In addition to the two pizzas that are always on our menu, we also do two specials: one meat special and one vegetarian option. Preparing for the specials takes anywhere from a few minutes to up to 12 hours for toppings like slow-roasted pork.

We open from 12:30 to 4:00, and during that time we typically make 150 pizzas. We also serve a salad, garlic bread, wine, coffee and apple juice. It might look frantic and disorganized when you walk in the door, but it works really well. Everything is self-service, so people are constantly milling around the room and kids are free to wander too. Someone might even play a little tune on the upright piano in the cookery school foyer. It all makes for a very casual, fun, family-friendly atmosphere.

We use the same playing card system I saw in the Cheese Board. When you order a pizza we give you a playing card, which we call out when your pizza is ready to be picked up. The happy hum in the room is constantly punctuated by the dinging bell and one of the staff calling out the cards: 'Queen of diamonds ready for pick-up! Five of clubs ready for pick-up!' This system has two major benefits: it means we don't need staff for table service and it's a bit of fun that makes people feel like a winner.

Saturday Pizzas at Home

Like any food business, we don't like to waste food. All our food scraps go to the cookery school's hens – believe it or not, they go mad for the leftover pizza crusts – and whatever they don't eat will eventually make its way to the compost bucket.

Saturday Pizzas at Home practically happened by accident. When we had some leftover pizzas one week, I wrapped them up in clingfilm/plastic wrap and stashed them in the freezer. And like most things that I stash in the freezer, I promptly forgot about them. Fast forward a few months and I wondered what had happened to those pizzas. I dug them out of the freezer and cooked them up, and they were fantastic.

After that, we made some extra pizzas one week, wrapped them up and sold them in the farm shop at the cookery school. They sold well there, so I asked a local petrol/gas station if they would be interested in selling them. They sold so many that they asked for more, and then more again. I could see that I was

on to something with this idea, so I reached out to a few more local shops and Saturday Pizzas at Home took off from there.

Soon we had so many shop orders and so many people coming through the door on Saturdays that we couldn't keep up, but I wasn't sure what direction to take this new aspect of the business in. I still felt like I was just the butcher's boy; I didn't know anything about business. Some people told me I should outsource the production of the pizzas and create a brand, but that would have meant losing control over the product and the quality and I didn't want that. Other people I talked to warned me away from that outsourcing idea, saying my product would just die a slow and lonely death on the shelf.

Around this time I went to New York to visit a friend and I did a butchery demo and a radio interview while I was there too. As I looked around the studio at Heritage Radio, I realized that we were in a shipping container (which also just so happens to be in the famous Roberta's Pizza restaurant). It was another eureka moment: I could set up a converted shipping container in the cookery school grounds and use it as a little pizza-making factory. So that's exactly what I did. When I got back from New York I asked our local builder where I could get a shipping container, and unbelievably, it turned out that his brother sells them. Within eight months we went from supplying half a dozen local shops to 19, including some of the bigger supermarkets, and we are continuing to grow.

Over the years we often had people ask if we would do home delivery or if they could pick up pizzas after closing time, so Saturday Pizzas at Home has become the ideal way for our customers to enjoy the same wood-fired Margherita and pepperoni pizzas that we serve at the weekly pop-up. It also means that Saturday Pizzas isn't just a Saturday job for me anymore – it has become a full-time business.

How to make a business out of pizza

1 Offer what people want to buy, not just what you like and want to sell. For example, if you think that Hawaiian pizza is the best pizza in the world, don't be surprised that not everybody thinks so too. In other words, if you're the only person that likes your product, then nobody is going to buy it.

2 Believe in the integrity of your business. People can tell when you're passionate about your product.

3 Work hard, but also work smart. Get a calculator and crunch the numbers, because the success of your business will be measured in them.

4 You need to have a system. If you're the best in your area of the business but only you can do it, how can you ever have time off and let somebody else take over for a little while? Systems make work easy.

5 Don't pursue perfection. Everybody makes mistakes, especially when setting up a new business, but the important thing is to learn from them. Try your best and give it all you've got, then next time, give a little more.

How to make great pizza

After nearly 10 years of making pizza, I wanted to share some of our favourite recipes as well as all the things I've learned along the way. But this book is also based on my mistakes. I've probably made every mistake possible – forgetting to put salt in the dough, using the wrong flour, putting too many toppings on the pizza, loading up the oven with damp wood – but I always learned from them and it has made me a better pizza maker in the end. This book will tell you how to do it right and also what to do when things go wrong.

The recipes in this book are a reflection of the local, seasonal ingredients available to us in East Cork and aren't set in stone. We use wild garlic when it's in season and rocket/arugula the rest of the year, we use thyme one week but marjoram the next, or we put rosé veal sausage on the menu when a calf from the farm's herd has been butchered. Use the recipes as a springboard for creating your own combinations of toppings, based on whatever you happen to have on hand yourself. The variations listed in many of the recipes will give you an idea of the endless different directions you can take your toppings in. For example, we often make a simple pizza of roast chicken, thyme and aioli, but towards the end of the summer we'll make a version with spring onions/scallions, homegrown sweetcorn and coriander/cilantro, whereas in the autumn we might use creamy spinach and rosemary instead.

When it comes to toppings, there are no rules. The main thing to keep in mind is balance. You don't want a pizza that's too cheesy or too saucy, nor do you want one that only has a few stingy slices of pepperoni or only a few olives. Try to get an even spread of toppings so that every slice has a little of everything.

But this book isn't just about the recipes. If you follow the principles, tips and techniques in this book, you will make great pizzas. But when you make them over and over again, you will master them. One of the things that cooking has taught me is that if you use these same principles of mastery through repetition in other areas of your life, you can achieve any goal you set for yourself.

GETTING STARTED

Equipment

You don't need any fancy or expensive equipment to make great pizza at home. There are plenty of gadgets and specialist equipment available on the market, such as high-end pizza stones made from ultra-conductive steel, but I bet you already have most, if not all, of what you need to get started.

Before you invest in any new kitchen equipment or gadgets, ask yourself if you're really going to get good use and value out of it or if it will quickly find its way to the back of the cupboard, never to see the light of day again. If you're willing to have it visible on your work surface or if you know you'll use it at least once a week, then it's a good buy.

Dough cutter and bowl scraper

A dough cutter is a vital piece of equipment. If you get nothing else, get one of these. In fact, I suggest you get two: a metal one for cutting the dough into portions and a plastic bowl scraper, which is a little more flexible and won't scratch surfaces. You can buy either one fairly cheaply at any good kitchen supply store or online, but if you make a lot of pizza or bread, it might just be the best investment you make in your kitchen this year.

Rolling pin

Even when you become a pro at stretching dough by hand there will inevitably be a few times when you'll have to roll it out instead because the dough is too delicate or too stiff to stretch it, so a sturdy rolling pin is a must.

Pizza stone, pizza pan or baking tray

The advantage of a pizza stone is that it retains heat well and conducts it evenly, resulting in a crispier base, but it's not essential. You can still get good results using a metal pizza pan that you can find in any kitchen

supply store. But failing that, you can also bake a pizza on a baking tray that you've turned upside down and preheated in the oven.

Pizza peel

A pizza peel or paddle is like a small flat shovel that's used for transferring pizzas in and out of the oven. Peels designed for home use have short handles, but peels to be used with wood-fired ovens have a very long handle so that you can slide the pizza close to the fire. If you don't have a pizza peel, then a thin wooden chopping board works well too. We sell a stainless steel pizza peel made by KitchenCraft in the shop at the cookery school. One advantage of a metal peel is that the pizza slides off it more easily than a wooden one, but a wooden peel can do double duty as a chopping board when your pizza comes out of the oven.

Pizza cutter

Proving the point that you don't need fancy equipment, we use a pizza cutter that I picked up in Ikea. The other type of cutter is a large double-handled pizza knife that looks like a giant mezzaluna and will cut a pizza all the way across in one clean slice.

Ladle

Did you know there are specific ladles for pizza? They have a flat base so that you can use the bottom to spread the sauce evenly over the dough, but a regular ladle or even a big metal spoon works fine for this too.

Pastry brush

You'll need a pastry brush for brushing the rim of the dough with olive oil. Just make sure that the hairs of the brush don't come off and stick to the dough. You might prefer to get a silicone brush for this reason.

Flour shaker

A flour shaker gives you a nice, light, even dusting of flour on your peel or chopping board and dough. This is especially important when you're working with wet, sticky dough.

Dough container

You'll need something to put your dough on or in while it rests and it needs to be something that can be kept covered at all times. Separate side plates for each ball of dough work really well and are easy to cover in clingfilm/plastic wrap and stash in your fridge, but a baking tray works too, as does a large airtight container with a lid. If using a baking tray, leave a good bit of space between the dough balls because they will spread out as they rest and if they merge together it will be hard to keep them in a nice round shape. If using an airtight container, you might be better off using separate ones for each ball of dough and use one that's big enough to let you manoeuvre in it to easily scoop out the dough ball while still maintaining its shape.

Digital kitchen scales

You'll get better and more consistent results if you weigh your ingredients, including water, rather than using measuring cups. Once you make the switch to digital kitchen scales, you'll never look back. All the recipes in this book work best if you weigh your ingredients.

Mortar and pestle

A good-quality stone mortar and pestle is a beautiful piece of kitchen equipment and will last a lifetime. I use it for crushing garlic into a paste, crushing herbs and grinding spices. You can even make mayonnaise in one. I did a cooking course in Thailand and the Thai chef said that an important part of using a mortar and pestle is to make lots of noise – he meant that to really work things into a paste, you can't be afraid of it!

Japanese mandoline

These are brilliant for slicing foods thinly, but use it carefully and always use the safety guard. The blade is razor sharp and it's all too easy to cut yourself.

Squeezy bottle

If you want to drizzle lines of mayonnaise on your pizzas – and believe me, once you try it, you'll be hooked – then a plastic squeezy bottle is a handy thing to have.

Ingredients

Strong white flour

Strong white flour has lots of gluten in it, which is what makes dough elastic. The high gluten content in strong white flour is perfect for pizza dough, pasta and bread, but not for more delicate things like cakes or pastry. At the pizzeria we use Doves Farm Organic Strong White Bio-bake Bread Flour, but you can use any flour labelled as strong or very strong, bread flour or 'oo' flour. 'oo' flour (which stands for *doppio zero*, or double zero) is an Italian flour used in pasta and pizza dough. The numbers are an indication of how finely the flour is ground – Italians use a scale from oo to 2 and 'oo' flour is almost like powder – and how much of the bran and germ have been removed. Every type or brand of flour will absorb a different amount of water, so every time you make dough it will be different, even if you're using the same recipe and doing everything the same way each time. Plus the more protein there is in the flour, the more water it will absorb. You need to use your judgment as to whether or not a particular batch of dough needs a little more flour or another splash of water. The more pizza dough you make, the better you will become at judging this.

Water

Tap and bottled water can differ in temperature, pH level, mineral content, and so on. The minerals in hard water make a more elastic dough, whereas acidic water weakens gluten and heavily chlorinated water can slow the growth of yeast. The most important factor, though, is that whatever water you use in your dough it must be safe and good to drink. Most tap water is fine, but if in doubt, filter it or use bottled water. When making pizza you want a wet, soft, sticky dough with lots of water because it will result in a lighter, crispier crust. A dry dough will result in a dense crust, which isn't what you want in a pizza. You can use cold or lukewarm water, but don't use hot water or it will kill the yeast. The temperature of the water will affect how active the yeast will be. If you want to use your dough fairly soon, without giving it a long rise, use lukewarm water to get the yeast going. If you'll be storing the dough in the fridge to let it ferment for any length of time, cold water is fine. Like most bakers, I prefer to weigh water, which gives you more accurate and consistent results. Simply put the mixing bowl on a kitchen scale and weigh the water first, then add all the dry ingredients. The handy thing about water is that its weight in millilitres is the same as its weight in grams, so it couldn't be easier to calculate: 100 ml of water = 100 g. When making any type of dough, it's always a good idea to keep back a little of the water (or whatever the main liquid ingredient is, such as milk or buttermilk) and see how the dough is coming together before adding the rest. You can always add more, but you can't take it out.

Salt

There are many different types of salt, such as sea salt (which can be flaky, fine or coarse), kosher salt, pink Himalayan salt and dairy salt. It's important to use the type of salt called for in a recipe, otherwise the ratio of salt to the other ingredients will be off. For example, 1 teaspoon of fine sea salt can have almost double the amount of salt as 1 teaspoon of flaky sea salt. Salt is added to pizza dough for flavour but also because it plays an important part in the structure and texture of dough. It makes the gluten more stretchy and thus it makes the dough stronger and more elastic, so use the amount and type called for in the recipe to get the best results.

Yeast

A living organism, yeast produces carbon dioxide, which is what makes dough light and airy. If you just mix together flour, water and salt without any yeast, it will be heavy and hard to digest. There are three types of yeast: fresh yeast, which you can buy in some specialist stores or baker supply stores; fast action dried yeast, which is widely available; and wild yeast, which is in the air all around us. You have to capture wild yeast with a mixture of flour and water – this is how you make a sourdough starter, like the one in our sourdough pizza recipe on page 28. We use fast action dried yeast in all our other doughs because it's easy to source and store.

Cheese

Mozzarella is the classic pizza cheese. It has a neutral flavour, which makes it an ideal base for other toppings. But all mozzarella is not created equal. Fresh, whole mozzarella or ready-grated mozzarella are the most widely available. Fresh can be made from water buffalo milk (*mozzarella di bufala*) or cow's milk (*fior di latte*) and it has more moisture than the grated mozzarella you can buy in bags at the grocery store, so it melts differently on a pizza. You can use many types of cheese on a pizza – just look at the classic *quattro formaggi* (four cheese) pizza for an example of that – but mozzarella is used as a basic topping for almost all the pizza recipes in this book. As with any other ingredient, use the best-quality mozzarella you can find to make the best pizzas.

Tomatoes

Whether you use fresh or canned tomatoes, the most important thing is that they are ripe and good quality. I recommend using good-quality cans of whole plum tomatoes, the gold standard being San Marzano tomatoes imported from Italy, if you can get them. The best tomatoes only need to be blended with some salt and pepper and maybe a pinch of sugar to balance out their acidity to make a delicious sauce, which is how Neapolitan pizzerias typically do it.

Olive oil

The first thing we do when assembling our pizzas is to brush the rims with olive oil before they go into the oven to help the crust turn golden. What type you use is up to you – you can use your regular, everyday olive oil that you cook with or you could use your premium extra virgin oil to add extra flavour.

Greens and fresh herbs

We love adding a handful of fresh greens or finely chopped fresh herbs to many of our pizzas. Lightly drizzle rocket/arugula, baby spinach and such like with olive oil and season with a pinch of salt and pepper before adding it to the pizza. This not only adds flavour, but the oil helps to prevent the greens from burning in the intense heat of the oven. You can either wilt greens briefly by adding them at the very end of the pizza's cooking time or add them after the pizza comes out of the oven to let them wilt in the residual heat. If you're going to put the greens back in the oven, only do so for 1 minute maximum and keep a close eye on them to make sure they don't burn. A top tip is to wash fresh herbs in a salad spinner, then store them in an airtight container lined with a piece of damp kitchen paper/paper towel to help keep them fresh for longer.

Ovens

The hotter the oven, the quicker the pizza will cook and the crispier it will get. Most domestic ovens can get up to 250°C/480°F/gas mark 9, whereas we cook our wood-fired pizzas at 450°C/840°F, which is why a wood-fired pizza can cook in as little as 2 or 3 minutes. Even though domestic ovens don't get nearly as hot as a wood-fired oven, you can still get great results from them. The key is to turn your oven up as hot as it gets, regardless of whether you have a conventional electric, fan-assisted electric or gas oven (though do note that all the recipes in this book were developed with a fan-assisted electric oven) and let it preheat for 1 hour to get good and hot. If your oven has one, use the fan setting so that the air circulates, which helps to cook the pizza more evenly. We use a wood-fired oven at the pop-up and in our retail business. If you've really caught the pizza-making bug, there are lots of companies out there selling wood-fired ovens or you can even buy a kit and build one yourself.

Top tips for great results

1 **Mise en place is a must.** It's a French term that means 'everything in its place'. Prep all your ingredients and put them in separate small bowls. It's such an important part of professional kitchens that some chefs have even been known to get 'mise en place' tattooed on their arms. Having all your ingredients and equipment ready to go means you can make pizza quickly, even if you're cooking for a crowd.

2 **Weigh or measure your ingredients carefully.** When making dough, it's a good idea to weigh all the ingredients separately rather than dumping them all in on top of each other in the mixing bowl in case you accidentally put in too much of something. Or at the very least, add the ingredients in separate small piles so that you can scoop out just that one ingredient.

3 **Don't forget to taste.** One of the things we see all the time at the cookery school is people forgetting to taste the food they're making before serving it. When it comes to pizza, this is particularly true of the sauce – it should taste really good on its own, before you put it on a pizza and load it up with toppings. So don't forget to taste and season as you go. If something doesn't taste quite right and you don't know what's missing, 95 per cent of the time it's salt. But if you're afraid of over-salting a dish, take a tablespoon out of whatever you're cooking and add a tiny pinch of salt to that spoonful. Taste it again and then you'll know if the whole dish needs more salt.

4 **Don't forget to brush the rim of the pizza with olive oil.** This adds a little extra flavour and will help the crust to turn golden. If you're using a wood-fired oven the oil might burn, so you'll need to keep a close eye on it.

5 **Confidence and speed are key when using a pizza peel to put a pizza in the oven.** If you hesitate, the pizza might stick to the peel or some of it might flop off the pizza stone or tray. If you're just starting to make your own pizzas and are worried about the possibility of ruining an entire pizza because it sticks to the peel or falls off the stone or baking tray, then try making some extra dough, stretching or rolling it out and practising with that before moving on to a complete pizza. But if you'd really rather not bother with this at all, you can use a pizza pan and assemble the pizza directly on it.

6 **Keep the heat in the oven.** Get the pizza in the oven as quickly as possible and close the door. Check it after 5 minutes to see how it's coming along and gauge how much more time it needs, but don't be tempted to keep opening the oven to peek at it and let all the precious heat escape, as it needs to be as hot as possible.

7 **Clean as you go.** Fill up your sink with hot soapy water and slide in your plates, utensils and bowls as you finish with them. When the last pizza is in the oven, you'll have time to load up the dishwasher and wipe down your work surfaces, leaving you with just a few plates and glasses to clean up at the end of dinner.

8 **Give some ingredients a head start.** You need to cook things like onions and peppers before adding them to a pizza, otherwise the texture won't be right – they'll be too crunchy because they didn't have enough time to cook through. Some meats also need to be at least partly cooked beforehand to make sure they are fully cooked through after their second blast in the oven, when they go on top of the pizza.

9 **Always allow the pizza to stand for at least 1 minute** once it comes out of the oven and before you slice it, or the cheese will be too runny and it's liable to slide off.

10 **Practice makes perfect.** If you make pizzas even just once a week, you'll soon develop an intuitive knack for it and you'll be surprised at how quickly you can cook them. After you've been making pizza for a while, you can have homemade pizza on the table in an hour from start to finish, which is practically the same amount of time that you'd be waiting for a takeaway.

Common mistakes and how to fix them

1 If your dough ball isn't round anymore once you've scraped it off the plates or tray for shaping, pat it back into a circular shape before you stretch or roll it. If it just won't co-operate, though, an oval pizza isn't the end of the world!

2 If your dough isn't stretching well, it probably means there wasn't enough liquid in it to start off with. Just roll it out this time, but next time you make dough, try adding an extra splash of water if you think it needs it.

3 The most common mistake people make is putting too much tomato sauce or cheese on the pizza – you want only a thin layer of sauce. About 80 ml (1/3 cup) of sauce for a 25 cm (10 in) pizza is usually plenty. If you want extra, serve it in a bowl on the side for dipping instead.

4 If your dough develops a small hole in it before you've added any toppings, pinch it back together as best you can. If it's only tiny, it will probably be fine. But if there's a hole in the dough that you didn't know about before you put it in the oven, watch out for melted cheese or spilled sauce on the pizza stone or baking tray if you'll be cooking other pizzas on it, as the other pizzas could stick and tear too when you slide them off.

5 Make sure there is no liquid on the peel or board, including olive oil or tomato sauce, or your pizza won't slide off it and the base could tear. Shake the peel or board gently to see if the pizza will move. If it doesn't, lift up the pizza with a dough cutter or spatula and sprinkle a little flour on the peel or board until it does move easily. The longer the dough sits around, the more it will stick. If the base has been sitting for a few minutes, give it a shake again to make sure it's moving easily before you add the toppings.

6 Leopard spots on a pizza – those charred, blackened bubbles on the crust – are a personal preference. If there's too much char on your pizza after it comes out of the oven (although this is more of an issue with wood-burning ovens than electric ovens), just scrape it off.

7 Pizza can go from cooked to burnt really quickly, so don't be tempted to squeeze in a quick task away from the kitchen. Watch it carefully after the 5-minute mark, setting the timer in 1-minute increments after that.

8 If you overshoot the pizza when sliding it onto the stone or baking tray and some of it is falling off the side, take the stone or pan out of the oven and try to shake it back on. Be aware of any ingredients that may have fallen off in the oven and clean them up when the oven is cold or clean them off the stone or tray right away so that the next pizza doesn't stick to it.

9 If your slice of pizza isn't coming away cleanly, it's because you haven't cut it all the way through. Pizza cutters get dull over time, so if this is a persistent problem, it might need to be replaced.

10 Some mistakes just can't be fixed. We inevitably drop a few pizzas during the course of a Saturday afternoon or some of them develop holes in the dough. There's nothing for it but to throw that one away and chalk it up to experience.

DOUGH + BREAD

Once you understand how dough is made and how it works, a world of possibilities will be open to you, from thin crust Neapolitan pizza to Chicago deep dish and everything in between. There are a lot of books out there that go into detail on the science behind making dough, but we're going to stick to the basics here, which is enough to get you making pizzeria-quality pizzas in your own home kitchen. And remember, when it comes to dough, practice makes perfect!

THE BASICS

The most important thing to realize when making dough is that every dough is different. Even if you're using the same recipe and the same brand or type of flour, it will change a little every time you make it. I make pizza almost every day, and every single pizza is different. The only way you'll be able to get consistent results is through practice. Once you know how your pizza dough is supposed to behave, you'll be able to judge if it needs another splash of water or an extra pinch of flour.

Almost all dough is made with four basic ingredients: flour, water, salt and yeast. Each of these can and will vary every time you make dough (see pages 16–17 for more information on these ingredients). Other factors affect dough too, such as humidity, temperature and even the growing season when the wheat was harvested, but we won't get into that here.

When you combine flour, water, yeast and salt and mix them together, you're developing the gluten into a web that will trap the air produced by the yeast while the dough ferments. The longer you knead dough, the more supple, springy and elastic it will be. Ten minutes of kneading is plenty, but you can knead it for up to 20 minutes. It's possible to over-knead, though, especially if you're using a mixer, so if your dough has become dense and tough, you've overdone it and will need to start again.

Weigh your ingredients

Any baker will tell you that the best way to make dough is to weigh the ingredients, including water, rather than measure them in cups. Cup measurements can be off by as much as 50 per cent depending on how tightly or loosely you pack the ingredients, but weighing is always accurate. If you plan on making pizza or bread regularly, digital kitchen scales are a worthwhile and inexpensive investment if you don't already own any. For all the recipes in this book, you will have the greatest success if you weigh the ingredients and follow the amounts given in grams and millilitres rather than cups.

When you weigh out your ingredients for dough, it's a good idea to measure all the ingredients separately in case you accidentally dump in too much of any one ingredient, which will be hard to remove from the mixing bowl if you've put everything in together at the same time.

How to make dough with a mixer

If you have a stand mixer, let the machine and electricity do the hard work for you! If you have kitchen scales, place the bowl of your stand mixer on the scales and set them to zero. Slowly pour in the water until you have the required amount, remembering that the weight of water is the same as it is in millilitres (for example, 100 ml = 100 g). Add the flour on top of the water, then add the yeast and salt in separate piles in case you need to take some back out. Alternatively, measure out all the ingredients in separate bowls and then combine them.

Fit the mixer with the dough hook and set a timer to mix for 10 minutes on a medium–low speed. For the first few minutes it will look shaggy and you might be worried that it won't come together, but at the end of the 10 minutes, the dough should be smooth, springy and slightly sticky. Check the dough after a couple of minutes,

though, to see how it's coming along. If it's really dry and isn't coming together, add another tablespoon of water. If it looks really wet, add another tablespoon of flour.

Dust a clean work surface lightly with flour and tip the dough out onto it. Knead it by hand (see below for kneading instructions) a few times to bring it together into a smooth, round ball that holds its shape well and springs back when you poke it. If it doesn't pass those tests, knead it for 1–2 minutes more. The dough is now ready to be cut into portions as per the recipe and rested.

How to make dough by hand

Kneading dough by hand requires a lot of elbow grease, so put on an apron, roll up your sleeves and prepare yourself for a bit of a workout.

First lightly dust a clean work surface with flour. Place the flour, yeast and salt in a large mixing bowl and stir to combine, then make a well in the centre and pour in the water. Using a wooden spoon, start mixing the dry ingredients into the water. Once it starts coming together into a shaggy mess and is getting too hard to stir, switch to using one hand to fold the dough over itself, giving the bowl a quarter turn each time you fold over the dough and making sure all the flour is being incorporated into the water.

After the dough has started to come together into a rough ball, tip it out onto the floured work surface. To knead the dough, press the heel of one hand into the middle of the dough, pushing it down and away from you, then fold it in half. With your other hand, rotate the dough a quarter turn, push it down and away from you again, then fold it in half again. Keep doing this for 10–15 minutes, until you have a smooth, round ball that holds its shape well and springs back when you poke it. If it doesn't pass those tests, knead it for 1–2 minutes more. The dough is now ready to be cut into portions, as per the recipe, and rested.

How to rest the dough

Once you've made the dough and cut it into portions, you need to let it rest. It's possible to roll out the dough and use it right away if you really have to, but the flavour won't be as good and it will be hard to work with, so if you're short of time you might be better off making the soda bread dough on page 35.

Put the dough balls on separate side plates or a baking tray dusted generously with flour, bearing in mind that the dough will spread as it rests, so make sure you use a plate or tray that's big enough to allow for that and don't put the dough balls too close together if you're putting two of them on one baking tray. Cover tightly with clingfilm/plastic wrap or soak a clean tea towel in cold running water from the tap, then wring it out really well – it should just be damp, not dripping wet – and cover the dough with the damp cloth. Place the plates or tray in the fridge for at least 6 hours, but ideally overnight or even up to 48 hours. This allows the dough to ferment, which makes it lighter and easier to digest and it really improves the flavour.

You can leave most of the dough recipes in this book in the fridge for up to 48 hours. A dough that has been fermenting for 48 hours has the best, most complex flavour, but it will be wetter and stickier, so be warned that it will be a little harder to work with and might need to be rolled out rather than stretched. Experiment with fermenting the dough for 24, 36 and 48 hours to see what works best for you. I make all my pizza dough at least 24 hours before I want to use it.

How to stretch dough by hand

The main advantage of stretching pizza dough by hand is that it keeps most of the air bubbles in the dough, which gives you a puffier crust than if you roll it out.

A good way to practise stretching dough by hand when you're just starting out is to make extra dough – for example, make enough for four or six pizzas instead of two (see page 27) – and see how big you can stretch the first ball of dough before it tears. This will give you confidence for the next ball of dough to do it right – and not to overdo it! Use the scraps from the ball of dough you experimented with to make breadsticks (page 40). In fact, before I opened the pizzeria, I made a big batch of dough and invited my first employees to my house so that everyone could practise stretching the dough. I reassured them that we weren't going to cook with the dough, so I encouraged them to really play around with it. I told them to throw it on the ground and up into the air and to try stretching it as far as it could go before the dough tore. By the time we opened the pizzeria, we were all stretching dough like pros.

Dust the pizza peel or a thin wooden chopping board with flour. The best way to do this is to use a flour shaker so that you get an even coating of flour.

Take the rested dough ball off the plate or tray using a dough cutter or bowl scraper, making sure the dough ball stays round. (I make all my pizzas into circles, but ovals or rectangles are fine too.) Place the dough ball on the floured peel or board and dust some flour on top of the dough too. Press down the middle of the dough with your fingers, but don't press the edge of the dough ball, as that will be the crust later. It should already look like a little pizza.

Lift up one edge of the dough and start to gently rotate it between your thumbs and index fingers. Gravity will stretch the dough and it will start to get bigger. If your dough was very wet to begin with this can happen quickly, but if your dough is a bit dry, you might have to pull it a bit. Dough has to be fairly wet to be stretched by hand, so if it's too dry and isn't co-operating at all when you try to stretch it, you'll have to roll it out instead.

Don't hold the dough too high up in front of you when you start to stretch it this way, otherwise gravity will work too well and it will stretch too much and too quickly.

Hold the dough lower down, closer to your work surface, rather than at eye level. In fact, it's fine if the bottom of the dough is resting on the work surface as you stretch out the top, constantly moving it around in a circle.

When the round of dough gets too big to continue stretching this way, make two fists with your hands and place the dough on top of your fists. Continue to rotate the dough using your knuckles, but now you can gently stretch the dough on the outside near the crust. The middle will continue to stretch itself. Once you're happy with the size of the dough (you should aim for 25 cm/10 in), place it back on the well-floured pizza peel or board. At this point, the dough is now ready for its toppings.

How to roll out dough

When you're in a hurry to make pizzas and have to use dough that hasn't had much time to rest, then rolling it out is your only option. Or if the dough isn't co-operating for whatever reason when you try to stretch it – maybe it's too wet and delicate, it's too dry, it's still too cold or it has risen too much – then rolling is also a better option than stretching.

An advantage of refrigerating dough is that chilling it makes it less elastic, which means it's less likely to spring back when you roll it out. Rolling dough is easier than stretching it, but the trade-off is that the crust will be uniformly flat, without the nice puffy crust of a hand-stretched dough.

Dust the pizza peel or wooden chopping board with flour. The best way to do this is to use a flour shaker so that you get an even coating of flour. Dust your rolling pin with plenty of flour too.

Take the dough ball off the plate or tray using a dough cutter or bowl scraper, making sure the dough ball stays round. (I make all my pizzas into circles, but ovals or rectangles are fine too.) Place the dough ball on the floured peel or board and dust some flour on top of the dough too. Press down the middle of the dough with your fingers. It should already look like a little pizza.

I find it works better to move your rolling pin up and down and to rotate the dough rather than roll it out side to side as well, so roll and rotate, roll and rotate until the dough is about 25 cm (10 in) in diameter. Dough can have an annoying habit of bouncing back when you try to roll it out, so press down firmly with the rolling pin.

Shake the peel or board gently to make sure the dough isn't sticking to it. If it is, use a dough cutter, bowl scraper or spatula to lift up the pizza and sprinkle a little flour on the peel or board until it does move easily. At this point, the dough is ready for its toppings.

How to freeze dough

After you've made your dough and portioned it into individual balls (but before you've stretched it or rolled it out), you can freeze it by tightly wrapping each ball separately in clingfilm/plastic wrap. To defrost a ball of dough, take it out of the freezer in the morning, unwrap it and place it on a plate, then cover tightly with clingfilm/plastic wrap again and let it thaw in the fridge. Let it sit out at room temperature for 1 hour before you want to cook it, then stretch it or roll it out as per usual. Dough can be frozen for up to six months.

Alternatively, you can assemble the pizza, bake it, allow it to cool and freeze the whole thing for up to six months. It will reheat in a hot oven in just 5 minutes. This is how we make our frozen pizzas for our retail business.

Want to learn more?

I teach several pizza-making masterclasses throughout the year at the cookery school. In a separate course, you can also learn how to make Italian breads such as focaccia, panzerotti, piadina, sfinciuni or carta di musica. Check the Ballymaloe Cookery School website for details: www.cookingisfun.ie.

CLASSIC PIZZA DOUGH

The beauty of this pizza dough is that it's wonderfully stretchy – you can even toss it in the air like a pizza-maker in Naples, which I do every now and then to impress the kids. This is the recipe I use for all the pizzas in the pizzeria and all our frozen pizzas. I like to use half 'oo' flour and half strong white flour, but you can use all of one or the other. Be warned, though, that if you use all 'oo' flour you will probably need to add a little extra, as otherwise it will be a very wet dough that might be hard to work with. I always make this dough at least 24 hours in advance of using it.

This recipe is also incredibly versatile. Using the same ingredients with just slight variations in the method, you can also make garlic bread (page 38), dough balls with garlic butter (page 37) and breadsticks (page 40).

200 ml (¾ cup + 4 tsp) cold water
300 g (2 cups) 'oo' flour or strong white flour, plus extra for dusting
½ x 7 g (¼ oz) sachet of fast action dried yeast
1 tsp fine sea salt

Makes enough for 2 x 25 cm (10 in) pizzas

Pour the water into the bowl of a stand mixer fitted with a dough hook, then add the flour on top of the water and add the yeast and salt in separate piles. Mix for 10 minutes on a medium–low speed. For the first few minutes it will look shaggy and you might be worried that it won't come together, but leave it be and by the end of the 10 minutes the dough should be smooth, springy and slightly sticky. Check the dough after a couple of minutes, though, to see how it's coming along. If it's really dry and isn't coming together, add another tablespoon of water. If it looks really wet, add another tablespoon of flour. Alternatively, if you don't have a mixer, you can knead the dough by hand (see pages 24–25).

Sprinkle your work surface with a little flour and tip the dough out onto it. Knead it by hand a few times to bring it together into a smooth, round ball that holds its shape well and springs back when you poke it. If it doesn't pass those tests, knead it for 1–2 minutes more.

Using a dough cutter or a sharp knife, cut the dough in half. Pressing it firmly into the work surface, roll each piece into a smooth round, like a tennis ball. Put the dough balls on two side plates or a baking tray dusted with flour. Cover tightly with clingfilm/plastic wrap or soak a clean tea towel in cold running water from the tap and wring it out really well, then cover the dough with the damp cloth. Place the covered plates or tray in the fridge for at least 6 hours, but ideally overnight or even up to 48 hours to let it have a long fermentation and a slow rise. The longer you let the dough sit in the fridge, the more flavour it will have.

Take the dough out of the fridge 1 hour before you want to cook the pizzas, making sure you keep it covered with the clingfilm/plastic wrap or damp cloth so it doesn't dry out. When you're ready to shape the dough, dust a pizza peel or a thin wooden chopping board generously with flour. You can either stretch the dough by hand or use a rolling pin. If you're using a rolling pin, dust that with flour too.

Take the rested dough ball off the plate or tray using a dough cutter or a bowl scraper, making sure the dough ball stays round at this point. Place the dough ball onto the floured peel or board and dust some flour on top of the dough too. Press down the middle of the dough with your fingers, but don't press the edge of the dough ball, as that will be the crust later. It should already look like a little pizza.

The dough is now ready to be stretched by hand or rolled out as per the instructions on pages 24–25.

This recipe makes two pizzas, but if you want to make more than that, here are the quantities to use for four or six pizzas. Even if you're only making two pizzas, you can still make a bigger batch and either freeze the leftover dough, ready to go for the next time you make pizza (see page 25 for tips on how to freeze dough), or you could make it into the recipes for garlic bread, dough balls with garlic butter and breadsticks later on in this chapter.

Makes 4 x 25 cm (10 in) pizzas
300 ml (1$\frac{1}{4}$ cups) cold water
500 g (3$\frac{1}{3}$ cups) '00' flour or strong white flour, plus extra for dusting
7 g ($\frac{1}{4}$ oz) sachet of fast action dried yeast
2 tsp fine sea salt

Makes 6 x 25 cm (10 in) pizzas
550 ml (2$\frac{1}{4}$ cups) cold water
950 g (6$\frac{1}{3}$ cups) '00' flour or strong white flour, plus extra for dusting
1$\frac{1}{2}$ x 7 g ($\frac{1}{4}$ oz) sachets of fast action dried yeast
1 tbsp fine sea salt

SOURDOUGH PIZZA DOUGH

Sourdough is the king of bread. Water, flour and wild yeast from the air combine to create a living culture – the most basic, ancient form of bread making. The most important aspect of this natural fermentation is the starter, also called leaven, sponge or starter culture. If you want to learn more about the science of sourdough, check out Andrew Whitley's book *Bread Matters*.

There are many different ways of making the starter, which takes a week to get going. Here at the cookery school we use a simple three-step method that Tim Allen, our resident bread expert, uses: starter, sponge, bread (or in our case, pizza dough). When you make a sourdough starter from scratch, don't be disappointed if your first few pizzas or loaves of bread are a bit flat – it takes a while for a starter to develop, so the more you use it, the better your dough will become.

For the starter:
120 ml (½ cup) lukewarm water
25 g (2 tbsp) rye flour
100 g (⅔ cup) strong white flour

For the sponge:
250 ml (1 cup) lukewarm water
250 g (1⅔ cups) strong white flour

For the dough:
100 ml (⅓ cup + 4 tsp) lukewarm water
375 g (2½ cups) strong white flour, plus extra for dusting
1½ tsp rye flour
1¼ tsp fine sea salt

Makes enough for 4 x 25 cm (10 in) pizzas

To make the starter, you'll need a large, airtight, non-reactive container (glass, plastic or ceramic). A large glass jar with a screw-top lid is ideal.

Day 1: Put 25 ml (5 tsp) of lukewarm water and 25 g (2 tbsp) of rye flour (rye flour is very good at attracting wild yeast) into the jar. Mix well with a wooden spoon, cover with the lid and leave at room temperature to ferment for 24 hours.

Day 2: Add 25 ml (5 tsp) of lukewarm water and 25 g (2 tbsp) of strong white flour to the jar. Mix well with a wooden spoon, cover with the lid and leave at room temperature to ferment for 24 hours.

Day 3: Add 25 ml (5 tsp) of lukewarm water and 25 g (2 tbsp) of strong white flour to the jar. Mix well with a wooden spoon, cover with the lid and leave at room temperature to ferment for 24 hours.

Day 4: Add 25 ml (5 tsp) of lukewarm water and 25 g (2 tbsp) of strong white flour to the jar. Mix well with a wooden spoon, cover with the lid and leave at room temperature to ferment for 24 hours.

Day 5: Add 25 ml (5 tsp) of lukewarm water and 25 g (2 tbsp) of strong white flour to the jar. Mix well with a wooden spoon, cover with the lid and leave at room temperature to ferment for 24 hours.

Day 6: Now you're ready to make the sponge. Transfer all of the starter into a large mixing bowl. Add 250 ml (1 cup) lukewarm water and 250 g (1⅔ cups) strong white flour and stir with a wooden spoon until well combined. Cover with clingfilm/plastic wrap and allow to ferment at room temperature for 24 hours. Clean the jar or container that you've been using for the starter because you'll need it again tomorrow.

Day 7: Take out 250 g (1 cup) of the sponge and put it back into the cleaned jar that you used for your starter. Close the lid and store in the fridge – this is your starter that you can use the next time you bake. When you want to make a new batch of dough, start at day 6 and use this starter to make the sponge. You should make a batch of sourdough fairly regularly to keep the starter going.

To make the dough, put the rest of the sponge into the bowl of a stand mixer fitted with a dough hook. You should have about 450 g (1 lb). Add 100 ml ($\frac{1}{3}$ cup + 4 teaspoons) water, then 375 g ($2\frac{1}{2}$ cups) strong white flour, $1\frac{1}{2}$ teaspoons of rye flour and $1\frac{1}{4}$ teaspoons of fine sea salt. Mix for 10 minutes on a medium–low speed. Check the dough after a couple of minutes to see how it's coming along – this tends to be a really wet dough, but if it's just too wet and looks more like a batter that isn't coming together into a ball, gradually add a little more flour until it comes away from the sides of the bowl. Alternatively, if you don't have a mixer, you can knead the dough by hand (see page 23).

Sprinkle your work surface generously with flour and tip the dough out onto it. Knead it by hand a few times to bring it together into a smooth, round ball. It may be softer than a typical dough but should still hold its shape well and spring back when you poke it. If it doesn't pass those tests, knead it for 1–2 minutes more. You might need to sprinkle over more flour if the dough is too wet or soft.

Using a dough cutter or a sharp knife, cut the dough in half, then cut in half again to make four equal pieces. Pressing it firmly into the work surface, roll each piece into a smooth round, like a tennis ball. Put the dough balls on four side plates or two baking trays dusted with flour. Cover tightly with clingfilm/plastic wrap or soak a clean tea towel in cold running water from the tap and wring it out really well, then cover the dough with the damp cloth. Place the covered plates or tray in the fridge for at least 6 hours, but ideally overnight or even up to 48 hours to let it have a long fermentation and a slow rise. The longer you let the dough sit in the fridge, the more flavour it will have.

Take the dough out of the fridge 1 hour before you want to cook the pizzas, making sure you keep it covered with the clingfilm/plastic wrap or damp cloth so it doesn't dry out. When you're ready to shape the dough, dust a pizza peel or a thin wooden chopping board with flour. You can either stretch the dough by hand or use a rolling pin. If you're using a rolling pin, dust that with flour too.

Take the rested dough ball off the plate or tray using a dough cutter or a bowl scraper, making sure the dough ball stays round at this point. Place the dough ball onto the floured peel or board and dust some flour on top of the dough too. Press down the middle of the dough with your fingers, but don't press the edge of the dough ball, as that will be the crust later. It should already look like a little pizza.

The dough is now ready to be stretched by hand or rolled out as per the instructions on pages 24–25.

SPELT PIZZA DOUGH

Spelt is an amazing grain. High in protein, fibre, vitamins and minerals, it's been an important source of nutrition since ancient times but has become popular again recently. Many people who suffer from gluten intolerance find that they can tolerate spelt, but spelt flour contains gluten so it's not suitable for those on a strict coeliac diet.

300 ml (1¼ cups) cold water

500 g (3½ cups) white spelt flour, plus extra for dusting

7 g (¼ oz) sachet of fast action dried yeast

2 tsp fine sea salt

Makes enough for 4 x 25 cm (10 in) pizzas

Pour the water into the bowl of a stand mixer fitted with a dough hook, then add the flour on top of the water and add the yeast and salt in separate piles. Mix for 10 minutes on a medium–low speed. For the first few minutes it will look shaggy and you might be worried that it won't come together, but leave it be and by the end of the 10 minutes the dough should be smooth, springy and slightly sticky. Check the dough after a couple of minutes, though, to see how it's coming along. If it's really dry and isn't coming together, add another tablespoon of water. If it looks really wet, add another tablespoon of flour. Alternatively, if you don't have a mixer, you can knead the dough by hand (see page 23).

Sprinkle your work surface with a little flour and tip the dough out onto it. Knead it by hand a few times to bring it together into a smooth, round ball that holds its shape well and springs back when you poke it. If it doesn't pass those tests, knead it for 1–2 minutes more.

Using a dough cutter or a sharp knife, cut the dough in half, then cut in half again to make four equal pieces. Pressing it firmly into the work surface, roll each piece into a smooth round, like a tennis ball. Put the dough balls on four side plates or two baking trays dusted with flour. Cover tightly with clingfilm/plastic

wrap. Place the covered plates or trays in the fridge for at least 6 hours, but ideally overnight. Be warned, though, that if you leave this dough overnight it's liable to be very wet and sticky, so you'd be better off rolling it out rather than stretching it by hand to avoid tearing it. The benefit of letting it ferment overnight is that you'll get a crispier dough.

Take the dough out of the fridge 1 hour before you want to cook the pizzas, making sure you keep it covered with the clingfilm/plastic wrap so it doesn't dry out. When you're ready to shape the dough, dust a pizza peel or a thin wooden chopping board generously with flour. Either stretch the dough by hand or use a rolling pin dusted with flour.

Take the rested dough ball off the plate or tray using a dough cutter or a bowl scraper, making sure the dough ball stays round at this point. Place the dough ball onto the floured peel or board and dust some flour on top of the dough too. Press down the middle of the dough with your fingers, but don't press the edge of the dough ball, as that will be the crust later. It should already look like a little pizza.

The dough is now ready to be stretched by hand or rolled out as per the instructions on pages 24–25. This dough tends to be stickier than the others, so rolling it out might be best.

WHOLEMEAL PIZZA DOUGH

If you like brown bread, you'll love this pizza dough. Ballymaloe House has been making their famous brown bread from Myrtle Allen's recipe for 60 years now. We make it in the cookery school every day and sell freshly baked loaves in the shop.

Wholemeal flour is what gives brown bread its distinctive taste and it has more vitamins and minerals than white because nothing is taken out. The wheat bran and germ are still in the flour, which makes it coarser than white flour, but it's also more nutritious and the dough is more filling. It also gives the dough a deeper brown colour.

300 ml (1¼ cups) cold water

250 g (1⅔ cups) strong wholemeal flour

250 g (1⅔ cups) strong white flour, plus extra for dusting

7 g (¼ oz) sachet of fast action dried yeast

2 tsp fine sea salt

Makes enough for 4 x 25 cm (10 in) pizzas

Pour the water into the bowl of a stand mixer fitted with a dough hook, then add the two flours on top of the water and add the yeast and salt in separate piles. Mix for 10 minutes on a medium–low speed. For the first few minutes it will look shaggy and you might be worried that it won't come together, but leave it be and by the end of the 10 minutes the dough should be smooth, springy and slightly sticky. Check the dough after a couple of minutes, though, to see how it's coming along. If it's really dry and isn't coming together, add another tablespoon of water. If it looks really wet, add another tablespoon of flour. Alternatively, if you don't have a mixer, knead the dough by hand (see page 23).

Sprinkle your work surface with a little flour and tip the dough out onto it. Knead it by hand a few times to bring it together into a smooth, round ball that holds its shape well and springs back when you poke it. If it doesn't pass those tests, knead it for 1–2 minutes more.

Using a dough cutter or a sharp knife, cut the dough in half, then cut in half again to make four equal pieces. Pressing it firmly into the work surface, roll each piece into a smooth round. Put the dough balls on four side plates or two baking trays dusted with flour. Cover tightly with clingfilm/plastic wrap. Place the covered plates or trays in the fridge for at least 6 hours, but ideally overnight.

Take the dough out of the fridge 1 hour before you want to cook the pizzas, making sure you keep it covered with the clingfilm/plastic wrap so it doesn't dry out. When you're ready to shape the dough, dust a pizza peel or a thin wooden chopping board with flour. You can either stretch the dough by hand or use a rolling pin dusted with flour.

Take the rested dough ball off the plate or tray using a dough cutter or bowl scraper, making sure the dough ball stays round at this point. Place the dough ball onto the floured peel or board and dust some flour on top of the dough too. Press down the middle of the dough with your fingers, but don't press the edge of the dough ball, as that will be the crust later. It should already look like a little pizza.

The dough is now ready to be stretched by hand or rolled out as per the instructions on pages 24–25.

IRISH STOUT PIZZA DOUGH

Ireland is famous for a certain stout, but in Cork we actually prefer the Beamish or Murphy's brands. These days we have many different locally brewed Irish craft stouts to choose from, such as Knockmealdown Stout from Eight Degrees Brewing in County Cork, Black Rock Irish Stout from the Dungarvan Brewing Company in County Waterford or Russian Imperial Stout from the White Gypsy Brewery in County Tipperary. Adding beer to pizza dough is a bit of fun, so use your favourite. The stout adds a tang and makes an extra-crispy crust if you let the dough ferment overnight.

180 ml (¾ cup) Irish stout
180 ml (¾ cup) cold water
500 g (3⅓ cups) strong white flour, plus extra for dusting
7 g (¼ oz) sachet of fast action dried yeast
2 tsp fine sea salt

Makes enough for 4 x 25 cm (10 in) pizzas

Carefully measure the stout so that you get the beer and not a cup full of foam. Pour the stout and water into the bowl of a stand mixer fitted with a dough hook, then add the flour on top of the liquid and add the yeast and salt in separate piles. Mix for 10 minutes on a medium–low speed. For the first few minutes it will look shaggy and you might be worried that it won't come together, but leave it be and by the end of the 10 minutes the dough should be smooth, springy and slightly sticky. Check the dough after a couple of minutes, to see how it's coming along. If it's really dry, add another tablespoon of water. If it looks really wet, add another tablespoon of flour. Or if you don't have a mixer, knead the dough by hand (see page 23).

Sprinkle your work surface with a little flour and tip the dough out onto it. Knead it by hand a few times to bring it together into a smooth, round ball that holds its shape well and springs back when you poke it. If it doesn't pass those tests, knead it for 1–2 minutes more.

Using a dough cutter or a sharp knife, cut the dough in half, then cut in half again to make four equal pieces. Pressing it firmly into the work surface, roll each piece into a smooth round. Put the dough balls on four side plates or two baking trays dusted with flour. Cover tightly with clingfilm/plastic wrap. Place the covered plates or trays in the fridge for at least 6 hours, but ideally overnight.

Take the dough out of the fridge 1 hour before you want to cook the pizzas, making sure you keep it covered with the clingfilm/plastic wrap so it doesn't dry out. When you're ready to shape the dough, dust a pizza peel or a thin wooden chopping board generously with flour. You can either stretch the dough by hand or use a rolling pin. If you're using a rolling pin, dust that with flour too.

Take the rested dough ball off the plate or tray using a dough cutter or a bowl scraper, making sure the dough ball stays round at this point. Place the dough ball onto the floured peel or board and dust some flour on top of the dough too. Press down the middle of the dough with your fingers, but don't press the edge of the dough ball, as that will be the crust later.

The dough is now ready to be stretched by hand or rolled out as per the instructions on pages 24–25.

RYE PIZZA DOUGH

Rye flour adds a good flavour and texture to pizza dough, but to keep the dough light you can't add too much of it. This is a good recipe to keep in mind if you ever find yourself with a little less strong white flour than you need for a batch of dough, as you can make it add up to 500 g/3⅓ cups with the inclusion of a little rye flour.

325 ml (1⅓ cups + 1 tsp) cold water

400 g (2⅔ cups) strong white flour, plus extra for dusting

100 g (⅔ cup) wholemeal rye flour

7 g (¼ oz) sachet of fast action dried yeast

2 tsp fine sea salt

Makes enough for 4 x 25 cm (10 in) pizzas

Pour the water into the bowl of a stand mixer fitted with a dough hook, then add the two flours on top of the water and add the yeast and salt in separate piles. Mix for 10 minutes on a medium–low speed. For the first few minutes it will look shaggy and you might be worried that it won't come together, but leave it be and by the end of the 10 minutes the dough should be smooth, springy and slightly sticky. This rye dough is a bit denser than the other doughs, so it won't be quite as springy. Check the dough after a couple of minutes, though, to see how it's coming along. If it's really dry and isn't coming together, add another tablespoon of water. If it looks really wet, add another tablespoon of flour. If you don't have a mixer, you can knead the dough by hand (see page 23).

Sprinkle your work surface with a little flour and tip the dough out onto it. Knead it by hand a few times to bring it together into a smooth, round ball that holds its shape well and springs back when you poke it. If it doesn't pass those tests, knead it for 1–2 minutes more.

Using a dough cutter or a sharp knife, cut the dough in half, then cut in half again to make four equal pieces. Pressing it firmly into the work surface, roll each piece into a smooth round, like a tennis ball. Put the dough balls on four side plates or two baking trays dusted with flour. Cover tightly with clingfilm/plastic wrap. Place the covered plates or trays in the fridge for at least 6 hours, but ideally overnight.

Take the dough out of the fridge 1 hour before you want to cook the pizzas, making sure you keep it covered with the clingfilm/plastic wrap so it doesn't dry out. When you're ready to shape the dough, dust a pizza peel or a thin wooden chopping board generously with flour. You can either stretch the dough by hand or use a rolling pin. If you're using a rolling pin, dust that with flour too.

Take the rested dough ball off the plate or tray using a dough cutter or a bowl scraper, making sure the dough ball stays round at this point. Place the dough ball onto the floured peel or board and dust some flour on top of the dough too. Press down the middle of the dough with your fingers, but don't press the edge of the dough ball, as that will be the crust later. It should already look like a little pizza.

The dough is now ready to be stretched by hand or rolled out as per the instructions on pages 24–25. This dough is a bit stiffer and drier than the others, so it takes more care and patience to stretch it.

GLUTEN-FREE PIZZA DOUGH

I had to experiment a lot to create a good gluten-free dough, but this is it. You need a few extra ingredients compared to a regular dough – eggs to bind the proteins, sugar to feed the yeast, vinegar to add acidity and some baking powder to help it all along. It can be chewier than the classic pizza dough, but the edges get nice and crispy.

This recipe makes a lot of dough, but I like to freeze it and have it on hand whenever a customer requests a gluten-free pizza. I roll out the dough and bake it with tomato sauce on top, then cool and freeze it on a paper plate wrapped in clingfilm/plastic wrap. We cook these straight from frozen in the high heat of our wood-fired oven. To cook it from frozen at home, defrost the base completely, in the fridge, first.

750 g (5 cups) gluten-free bread flour (we use Doves Farm), plus extra for dusting
7 g (¼ oz) sachet of fast action dried yeast
1 tsp fine sea salt
1 tsp sugar
½ tsp gluten-free baking powder
2 eggs, lightly beaten
300 ml (1¼ cups) lukewarm water
1 tbsp white wine vinegar
olive oil (optional)

Makes enough for 6 x 25 cm (10 in) pizzas

Place all the dry ingredients in the bowl of a stand mixer fitted with a dough hook and mix together. Add the eggs, water and vinegar and mix everything together on a medium–low speed for about 3 minutes, until it's starting to come together in a soft ball. If you don't have a stand mixer, you can just do this by hand.

Sprinkle a generous amount of gluten-free flour onto your work surface, your rolling pin and the ball of dough, then tip the dough out onto the work surface. You don't have to knead it thoroughly as you aren't developing any gluten – just knead it enough to bring it together.

Divide the dough into six equal pieces (about 200 g/7 oz each). Shape each piece into a fat disc about 10 cm (4 in) in diameter, then place on plates or baking trays, cover with a damp tea towel and leave to rest for 30 minutes.

To make your pizzas you can't stretch this dough by hand, so you need to roll it out – think of it as being more like a crumbly pastry dough than a regular yeast dough. Put the dough onto a well-floured pizza peel or a thin wooden chopping board. Dust the dough and the rolling pin with more flour. You need to use plenty of flour for dusting everything when making this gluten-free dough, so be generous and make sure you use the gluten-free flour for dusting.

Gently roll out each piece of dough until it's a thin base about 25 cm (10 in) in diameter, carefully lifting it now and then with a dough cutter, bowl scraper or spatula to make sure it's not sticking and dusting the top often with flour, because this dough will stick to both the board and the rolling pin. If it does break, try patching the dough back together with a little dab of olive oil or some of the offcuts if you trim it. If the edges have cracked and the base is looking a little ragged, you can trim it into a neat circle using the tip of sharp knife and the rim of a plate as a guide.

The dough is now ready to be finished with any toppings you want and baked like any of the other recipes in this book.

SODA BREAD PIZZA DOUGH

The first time I heard of a soda bread pizza I thought it would be stodgy and dense, but it actually works surprisingly well. It's rolled so thinly and bakes so quickly that it stays light. If you don't have any strong white flour in the house but still want to make pizza, this is the dough for you. Another advantage is that it takes only minutes to make and is ready to use right away without needing to rest, perfect for those times when you haven't planned ahead. Unorthodox and untraditional? Absolutely, but it will do in a pinch.

450 g (3¾ cups) plain/
   all-purpose flour, plus
   extra for dusting
1 tsp baking soda
1 tsp fine sea salt
400 ml (1⅔ cups)
   buttermilk

*Makes enough for
4 x 25 cm (10 in)
pizzas*

Sift the flour, baking soda and salt into a large mixing bowl and stir to combine. Make a well in the centre and pour in most of the buttermilk. Holding one hand in an open claw shape, use your fingers to mix the dry ingredients into the buttermilk. Add the remaining buttermilk if necessary and keep mixing until the dough comes together into a ball.

Sprinkle your work surface with a little flour and tip the dough out onto it. Wash your hands, then pat the dough into a round ball but try not to knead it, otherwise the dough will be tough. Using a dough cutter or a sharp knife, cut the dough in half, then cut in half again to make four equal pieces.

Dust a pizza peel or a thin wooden chopping board generously with flour and dust a rolling pin with flour too (you can't stretch this dough by hand). Use plenty of flour here, as this dough tends to stick. Place a piece of dough on the floured peel or board and dust plenty of flour on top of the dough too. Roll the dough out into a 25 cm (10 in) circle, stopping to dust the rolling pin with extra flour if it's starting to stick, which it probably will. Shake the peel or board to make sure the dough isn't sticking to it, then add your toppings and bake as per any of the pizza recipes in this book.

CHOCOLATE PIZZA DOUGH

One day I was walking through the kitchens at the cookery school and noticed one of the students experimenting with a chocolate bread dough. I liked the idea so much that I just had to try it myself to make into a dessert pizza.

375 ml (1½ cups + 1 tbsp) whole milk

475 g (3 cups + 2 tbsp) strong white flour, plus extra for dusting

100 g (½ cup) chocolate chips

25 g (2 tbsp) unsweetened cocoa powder

25 g (2 tbsp) drinking chocolate

7 g (¼ oz) sachet of fast action dried yeast

1 tbsp sugar

1 tsp fine sea salt

Makes enough for 4 x 25 cm (10 in) pizzas

Pour the milk into the bowl of a stand mixer fitted with a dough hook, then add the rest of the ingredients. Mix for 10 minutes on a medium–low speed. For the first few minutes it will look shaggy and you might be worried that it won't come together, but leave it be and by the end of the 10 minutes the dough should be smooth, springy and slightly sticky. Check the dough after a couple of minutes, though, to see how it's coming along. If it's really dry and isn't coming together, add another tablespoon of milk. If it looks really wet, add another tablespoon of flour. Alternatively, if you don't have a mixer, you can knead the dough by hand (see page 23).

Sprinkle your work surface with a little flour and tip the dough out onto it. Knead it by hand a few times to bring it together into a smooth, round ball that holds its shape well and springs back when you poke it. If it doesn't pass those tests, knead it for 1–2 minutes more. Don't worry if some of the chocolate chips are sticking out of the dough.

Using a dough cutter or a sharp knife, cut the dough in half, then cut in half again to make four equal pieces. Pressing it firmly into the work surface, roll each piece into a smooth round, like a tennis ball. Put the dough balls on four side plates or two baking trays dusted with

flour. Cover tightly with clingfilm/plastic wrap or soak a clean tea towel in cold running water from the tap and wring it out really well, then cover the dough with the damp cloth. Place the covered plates or trays in the fridge for at least 6 hours, but ideally overnight or even up to 48 hours to let it have a long fermentation and a slow rise. The longer you let the dough sit in the fridge, the more flavour it will have.

Take the dough out of the fridge 1 hour before you want to cook the pizzas, making sure you keep it covered with the clingfilm/plastic wrap or damp cloth so it doesn't dry out. When you're ready to shape the dough, dust a pizza peel or a thin wooden chopping board with flour and dust a rolling pin too, as this dough is too stiff and dry to be stretched by hand and needs to be rolled out.

Take the rested dough ball off the plate or tray using a dough cutter or a bowl scraper, making sure the dough ball stays round at this point. Place the dough ball onto the floured peel or board and dust some flour on top of the dough too. Press down the middle of the dough with your fingers – it should already look like a little pizza.

The dough is now ready to be rolled out as per the instructions on pages 24–25.

DOUGH BALLS WITH GARLIC BUTTER

These are like a variation on garlic bread and can be served as a side for pizzas, soup, pasta, salads or just about anything, really.

300 ml (1¼ cups) lukewarm water

500 g (3⅓ cups) strong white flour, plus extra for dusting

7 g (¼ oz) sachet of fast action dried yeast

2 tsp fine sea salt

olive oil, for greasing

60 g (4 tbsp) butter

2–3 garlic cloves, crushed

1 tbsp finely chopped fresh flat-leaf parsley, to garnish

Makes 16 balls

Pour the water into the bowl of a stand mixer fitted with a dough hook, then add the flour on top of the water and add the yeast and salt in separate piles. Mix for 10 minutes on a medium–low speed. For the first few minutes it will look shaggy and you might be worried that it won't come together, but leave it alone and by the end of the 10 minutes the dough should be smooth, springy and slightly sticky. Check the dough after a couple of minutes, though, to see how it's coming along. If it's really dry and isn't coming together, add another tablespoon of water. If it looks really wet, add another tablespoon of flour. Alternatively, if you don't have a mixer, you can knead the dough by hand (see page 23).

Sprinkle your work surface with a little flour and tip the dough out onto it. Knead it by hand a few times to bring it together into a smooth, round ball that holds its shape well and springs back when you poke it. If it doesn't pass those tests, knead it for 1–2 minutes more.

Lightly brush a large mixing bowl with a little olive oil. Place the ball of dough in the bowl and turn it to coat it all in the oil. Put it back in the bowl, seam side down, and cover with clingfilm/plastic wrap. Set aside in a warm place for 1½–2 hours, until the dough has doubled in size.

Line a large baking tray with non-stick baking paper and dust a clean work surface with flour.

Using your fist, punch down the risen dough and tip it out onto the floured work surface. Knead it by hand for 1 minute, then divide into 16 equal portions (40–50 g/1½–1¾ oz each is a good size to aim for) and roll or knead each one into a smooth, round ball. Place the balls on the lined baking tray and cover with a clean tea towel. Allow to rise again for about 30 minutes, until the balls are starting to join together (they will rise a little more when you bake them in the oven, so don't be tempted to let them rise too much now).

While the dough is rising the second time, preheat the oven to 200°C/400°F/ gas mark 6.

Place the butter and garlic in a small pan over a medium heat to melt the butter.

When the dough has had its second rise, remove the towel and brush the tops of the dough balls with about half of the garlic butter, trying to get all the bits of crushed garlic. Place the tray in the oven and bake the dough balls for 15–20 minutes, until the tops are golden and the base sounds hollow when you tap one.

Remove from the oven and brush with the remaining melted butter, then sprinkle over the chopped parsley. Allow to cool on a wire rack for a few minutes before tearing the balls apart and serving warm.

GARLIC BREAD

We didn't have garlic bread on our menu when we first started the pizzeria but people kept ordering it anyway, so now we make two different types. The first one has garlic only and the other one is a cheesy version with mozzarella (see the variation). Sometimes it seems like it's even more popular than the pizzas.

3 tbsp finely grated
    Parmesan
1 tbsp finely chopped
    fresh flat-leaf parsley
3 tbsp olive oil
2–3 garlic cloves, crushed
2 balls of classic pizza
    dough (page 26)

*Makes 2 x 25 cm
(10 in) rounds*

Preheat the oven to 240°C/475°F/gas mark 9 or as high as it will go. Place a pizza stone or an upside-down baking tray into the oven to heat up too. Get all your ingredients and equipment ready.

Place the grated Parmesan and chopped parsley in a bowl and mix together until well combined. Place the olive oil in a separate small bowl and stir in the crushed garlic.

Stretch the pizza dough by hand or roll out as per the instructions on pages 24–25. Using a pastry brush, generously brush the garlic-infused olive oil all over the dough, making sure bits of the crushed garlic are evenly scattered across the base.

Make sure there is no liquid on the peel or board or the garlic bread won't slide off it. Shake the board gently to see if the bread will move. If it doesn't, lift it up with a dough cutter, bowl scraper or spatula and sprinkle a little flour on the board until it does move easily.

Slide the garlic bread off the peel or board onto the pizza stone or upside-down baking tray in the hot oven. Cook for about 7 minutes – you want the bottom and the crust to be cooked through and golden but you don't want the garlic to burn, which will make it bitter.

Take the garlic bread out of the oven and transfer to a wire cooling rack, then sprinkle over the Parmesan and parsley mixture. Allow to stand for 1 minute before cutting into slices.

VARIATION

Cheesy garlic bread

Make the bread as per the recipe above, but divide 250 g (2 cups) of grated mozzarella between the two bases after you've brushed them all over with the garlicky olive oil and cook for 7–10 minutes, until the cheese has melted.

BREADSTICKS

This is the same recipe as the classic pizza dough on page 26, so if you ever have a little pizza dough left over, don't throw it away – make it into a few breadsticks instead. This recipe makes eight breadsticks, but if you want to make more, use the amounts for four or six pizzas on page 27.

- 200 ml (¾ cup + 4 tsp) lukewarm water
- 300 g (2 cups) strong white flour, plus extra for dusting
- ½ x 7 g (¼ oz) sachet of fast action dried yeast
- 1 tsp fine sea salt

Choice of toppings:
- 1 egg, lightly beaten
- poppy seeds
- sesame seeds
- finely grated Parmesan
- olive oil
- flaky sea salt and freshly ground black pepper
- melted garlic butter (page 37)

Makes 8

Pour the water into the bowl of a stand mixer fitted with a dough hook, then add the flour on top of the water and add the yeast and salt in separate piles. Mix for 10 minutes on a medium–low speed. For the first few minutes it will look shaggy and you might be worried that it won't come together, but leave it be and by the end of the 10 minutes the dough should be smooth, springy and slightly sticky. Check the dough after a couple of minutes, though, to see how it's coming along. If it's really dry and isn't coming together, add another tablespoon of water. If it looks really wet, add another tablespoon of flour. Alternatively, if you don't have a mixer, you can knead the dough by hand (see page 23).

Sprinkle your work surface with a little flour and tip the dough out onto it. Knead it by hand a few times to bring it together into a smooth, round ball that holds its shape well and springs back when you poke it. If it doesn't pass those tests, knead it for 1–2 minutes more.

Using a dough cutter or a sharp knife, cut the dough in half, then cut each piece into quarters so that you have eight evenly sized pieces of dough.

Use your hands to roll out each portion on the work surface into a long, thin sausage shape about 30 cm (12 in) long. Place on a baking tray lined with non-stick baking paper and brush lightly with the beaten egg, then sprinkle all over with poppy seeds, sesame seeds or finely grated Parmesan. Or skip the egg wash and brush with olive oil and sprinkle with big pinches of flaky sea salt and freshly ground black pepper or brush with some melted garlic butter. Or you could do a few of each. Cover the tray with a clean tea towel and let the breadsticks rise in a warm, draught-free place for 30 minutes.

Preheat the oven to 200°C/400°F/gas mark 6.

Remove the tea towel and bake the breadsticks in the oven for 15–20 minutes, until golden brown and cooked through. Allow to cool slightly on a wire rack, then serve while still warm.

These are best eaten on the day that they're made (otherwise they get very chewy), but they can be kept in an airtight container for a day or two and reheated in a warm oven (180°C/350°F/gas mark 4) for 5 minutes.

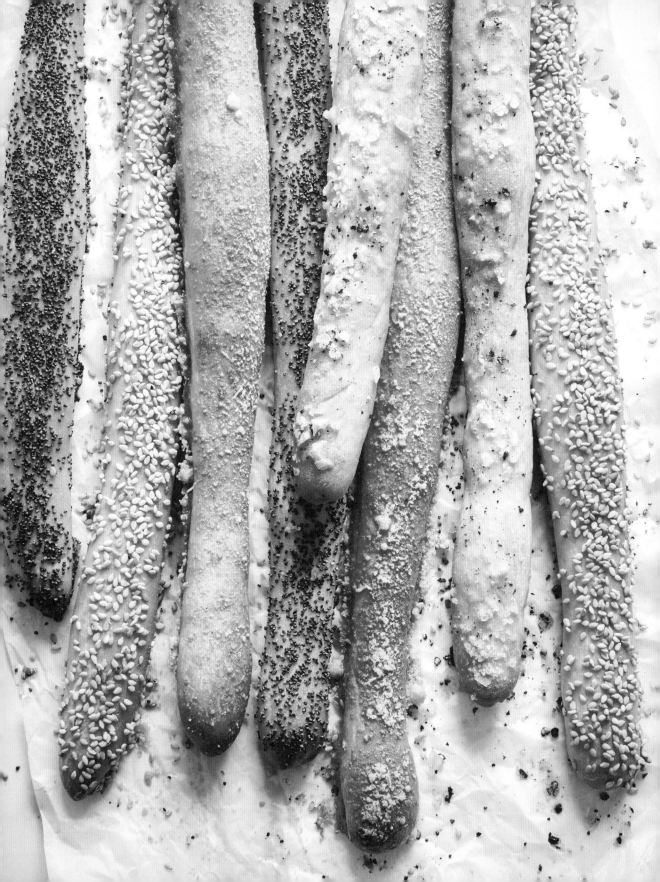

SAUCES + EXTRAS

Don't underestimate the importance of the sauce on a pizza. In addition to the base sauce, we often drizzle one or two extra sauces on top of the pizza at the end – two sauces are better than one! All the sauces are also ideal for dipping the crusts into if you want to serve extra on the side. I especially love eating the Béarnaise sauce on page 48 and the tapenade on page 55 this way. The extras like gremolata, pesto or pickled red onions are added after the pizza comes out of the oven to keep their freshness and vibrancy and to add a pop of colour.

The recipes in this chapter make more than you'll need for two pizzas, but you'll find loads of uses for them in other dishes throughout the week, so you'll be happy to have jars of homemade mayonnaise, caramelized onions, peperonata or chilli oil on hand. Most of the sauces freeze well too, so you might even want to make a double batch. And don't forget to taste and season as you go – the sauces in particular should be delicious on their own, just as they are, before you add them to a pizza.

TOMATO SAUCE

This sauce is so versatile. Not only can you use it for pizzas, but it works well as a simple pasta sauce too and it can be frozen for up to six months. Freeze it in ice cube trays for handy portions – just pop the cubes out and store them in a food bag, then take out only what you need and let them thaw ahead of time. But if time is tight, you can make a perfectly good sauce simply by blending a can of good-quality whole plum tomatoes with some salt, sugar and freshly ground black pepper, which is what pizza-makers in Naples do.

1 tbsp olive oil
1 onion, finely chopped
1 celery stick, finely chopped
½ carrot, finely chopped
1 tsp fine sea salt
freshly ground black pepper
1 garlic clove, finely chopped
2 x 400 g (14 oz) cans of good-quality whole plum tomatoes
1 tsp sugar (optional)

Makes 800 ml (3⅓ cups)

Heat the olive oil in a saucepan set over a medium–low heat. Add the onion, celery and carrot and season with the salt and some freshly ground black pepper to taste. Cover the pan and sweat the vegetables for 8–10 minutes, until soft but not coloured. Add the garlic and cook, uncovered, for just 1 minute, until fragrant. Add the tomatoes and simmer for 3 minutes on a low heat. Good-quality canned tomatoes don't need to be cooked for very long, plus the longer you cook the sauce, the more water evaporates and the thicker it becomes, which isn't the consistency that you want – pizza sauce should be thin but not watery.

Whizz the sauce with a hand-held blender until smooth, or you could leave it a little chunkier if that's what you prefer. Taste and check for seasoning – add a teaspoon of sugar if the tomatoes are too bitter or acidic. The sauce is now ready to be used right away, or it will keep in the fridge in an airtight container for up to a week or it can be frozen for up to six months (see the note above). This recipe makes enough sauce for five pizzas.

BBQ SAUCE

This BBQ sauce is delicious just as it is and is quick and easy to make, but if you're making the braised beef pizza on page 106, adding the beef cooking juices to the sauce instead of the water really takes it up a notch. My nephew Joshua absolutely adores this sauce.

200 ml (¾ cup + 4 tsp) tomato ketchup
100 ml (⅓ cup + 4 tsp) water
1 tbsp dark brown sugar
1 tbsp Worcestershire sauce
1 tsp red wine vinegar
½ tsp paprika
¼ tsp mustard powder
fine sea salt and freshly ground black pepper

Makes 240 ml (1 cup)

Put all the ingredients in a small saucepan and bring to the boil, then take off the heat. Allow to cool, then transfer to an airtight jar and store in the fridge for up to a week.

HOISIN SAUCE

Hoisin sauce is a versatile Chinese sauce that is often used as a glaze or marinade and served with pork, duck or chicken. My homemade version isn't as thick as the shop-bought ones, but it's just right for drizzling on the roast duck pizza on page 109.

2 tbsp smooth peanut butter
2 tbsp soy sauce
2 tsp dark brown sugar
2 tsp rice wine or white
  wine vinegar

1 garlic clove, crushed
freshly ground black pepper

Makes 80 ml (⅓ cup)

Whisk all the ingredients together in a jar until well combined. This will keep in the fridge, covered, for up to two weeks, but you may need to whisk it again before using if the ingredients have separated.

BÉCHAMEL SAUCE

This simple, plain sauce is a nice substitute for the usual tomato sauce, especially for pizzas with more delicate flavours, like the asparagus pizza on page 94 or the broad bean pizza on page 132, but it also works well on the spicy sausage pizza on page 79. Plus all the ingredients are probably things you always have on hand. This makes more than you'll need for two pizzas, but you can use the rest to make a lasagne the next day or try stirring the leftovers into mashed potatoes. Alternatively, just reduce the amounts here by half.

480 ml (2 cups) whole milk
1 carrot, sliced
½ onion, sliced
1 sprig of fresh parsley
1 sprig of fresh thyme
1 bay leaf
5 black peppercorns
30 g (2 tbsp) butter
30 g (¼ cup) plain/
  all-purpose flour
50 g (1 cup) finely grated
  Parmesan (optional)

*Makes 400 ml
(1⅔ cups)*

Pour the milk into a large saucepan, then add the carrot, onion, herbs and peppercorns. Bring the milk to the boil, keeping a close eye on the pan to make sure the milk doesn't boil over. Reduce the heat and gently simmer for 3–4 minutes. Remove the pan from the heat, cover with a lid and leave to infuse for 10 minutes.

Meanwhile, to make the roux, melt the butter in a small pan, then stir in the flour and cook them together on a low heat for 2 minutes, stirring occasionally.

Pour the milk through a fine-mesh sieve to strain out the vegetables and herbs, then bring it back to the boil. Once it's boiling again, whisk in the roux to thicken it. Add the Parmesan, if using, for a bit more pizza flavour.

You can store any leftovers in an airtight container in the fridge for up to five days, but you may need to thin it with a little more milk before using.

FENNEL SAUCE

This makes more than you'll need for two pizzas, but you can freeze the leftovers in an ice cube tray, then pop the cubes into a freezer bag, ready for the next time you want to use this sauce on a pizza. Or you could use it as a pasta sauce with plenty of grated Parmesan and some chopped fresh parsley.

If you're going to use a food processor to blend the cooked sauce, use the slicing attachment to cut the fennel and onion to make short work of the job.

1 tbsp olive oil
3 fennel bulbs, thinly sliced
1 onion, thinly sliced
1 garlic clove, thinly sliced
180 ml (¾ cup) white wine
480–720 ml (2–3 cups) vegetable or chicken stock
3 bay leaves
fine sea salt and freshly ground black pepper

*Makes 600 ml
(2½ cups)*

Heat the olive oil in a saucepan set over a medium–low heat. Add the fennel and onion, cover with a lid and sweat for 8–10 minutes, until the vegetables are soft. Add the garlic and cook, uncovered, for just 1 minute, until fragrant.

Pour in the wine and bring to the boil. Let it bubble up for 1 minute, then add 480 ml (2 cups) of the stock, the bay leaves and some salt and pepper. Reduce the heat and gently simmer for about 20 minutes, uncovered, until the fennel is completely soft. Remove the bay leaves and discard.

Transfer the sauce to a blender or food processor and liquidize until it is completely smooth. Check the consistency – if you'd like the sauce to be a little thinner, add some or all of the remaining 240 ml (1 cup) of stock and blend again. On the other hand, if it's too thin, put it back over a high heat and let it reduce until it's the consistency you want. Taste and adjust the seasoning if necessary.

Store leftovers in an airtight container in the fridge for up to one week or in the freezer for up to six months (see the note above).

HOLLANDAISE SAUCE

Making an emulsion sauce is a cooking technique that everyone should learn, and there's no better place to start than with hollandaise, one of the five French mother sauces. Like homemade mayonnaise (page 50), hollandaise takes only minutes to make.

2 egg yolks
2 tsp cold water
150 g (10 tbsp) cold butter, cut into sugar cube-size pieces
1 tsp freshly squeezed lemon juice

Makes 180 ml (¾ cup)

Put the egg yolks and water in a saucepan set over a low heat and whisk well. Add the butter bit by bit, whisking all the time. As soon as one piece of butter melts, add another piece. It will gradually thicken. You're aiming for a consistency like custard. Make sure the pan doesn't get too hot or the sauce will scramble. You should always be able to touch the side of the saucepan with your hand. If the pan is getting too hot, just slide it off the heat for a moment while continuing to whisk. Once all the butter has been incorporated, whisk in the lemon juice.

Hollandaise is famously tricky to keep warm or make ahead of time – it's an emulsion sauce, so it's in danger of splitting – so it's best used right away.

BÉARNAISE SAUCE

Béarnaise is a variation on hollandaise, so once you've mastered how to make it, you don't have to stick to the original ingredients. You can use onions instead of shallots or you can use parsley or any other herb instead of tarragon. It all depends on what you like or what ingredients you have to hand.

4 tbsp tarragon vinegar or white wine vinegar
4 tbsp dry white wine
2 tsp finely chopped shallot or onion
1 tbsp water
2 egg yolks
150 g (10 tbsp) cold butter, cut into sugar cube-size pieces
1 tbsp chopped fresh French tarragon

Makes 180 ml (¾ cup)

Put the vinegar, wine and shallot or onion into a saucepan. Bring to the boil and cook until the liquid has almost completely evaporated and the pan is almost dry but not brown. Add the tablespoon of water, remove the pan from the heat and cool for 1–2 minutes.

Whisk in the egg yolks and add the butter bit by bit over a very low heat, whisking all the time. As soon as one piece of butter melts, add another piece. It will gradually thicken. Make sure the pan doesn't get too hot or the sauce will scramble. You should always be able to touch the side of the saucepan with your hand. If the pan is getting too hot, just slide it off the heat for a moment while continuing to whisk. Once all the butter has been incorporated, add the tarragon.

Like hollandaise, Béarnaise is hard to keep warm or make ahead of time, so it's best used right away.

HOMEMADE RICOTTA

This is the easiest cheese to make at home – the only specialist equipment you need is a piece of cheesecloth or muslin. A simple ricotta (which means 'recooked') is traditionally made by reboiling the whey, and the curds that form are the cheese. Once you've made your own, you'll never buy ricotta from the shops again.

2.4 litres (10 cups) whole milk
240 ml (1 cup) single/light cream
½ tsp fine sea salt
2–3 tbsp freshly squeezed lemon juice

Makes 750 g (3 cups)

Put the milk, cream and salt into a large heavy-bottomed saucepan with high sides (a stock pot is good for this) and bring slowly to the boil over a medium heat, stirring occasionally with a wooden spoon.

Meanwhile, line a large sieve with cheesecloth or a double thickness of muslin. When the milk reaches a rolling boil, add the lemon juice and reduce the heat to low. Stir constantly for about 5 minutes, until the mixture curdles.

Gently pour the mixture into the lined sieve and allow to drain for about 1 hour. Discard the whey (we feed it to the chickens) and cool the ricotta, then chill in an airtight container in the fridge. It will keep fresh for two to three days.

MAYONNAISE

Mayonnaise on a pizza? I know it sounds crazy, but trust me, it works! We add a drizzle of mayonnaise to a lot of our pizzas when they come out of the oven to add an extra dimension of flavour. Never cook mayonnaise on a pizza, though, because it's an emulsion sauce and will split in the heat of the oven and look scrambled.

The secret to great mayonnaise is to have all your ingredients at room temperature and to drip the oil very slowly into the egg yolks at the beginning. The quality of your mayonnaise depends on the quality of your egg yolks, oil and vinegar – it's perfectly possible to make a bland mayonnaise if you use poor-quality ingredients.

2 egg yolks, preferably organic and free-range, at room temperature
2 tsp white wine vinegar
¼ tsp fine sea salt
¼ tsp Dijon mustard or a pinch of dry English mustard
180 ml (¾ cup) sunflower oil
60 ml (¼ cup) olive oil
1–2 tbsp water

Makes 300 ml (1¼ cups)

Put the egg yolks into a bowl with the vinegar, salt and mustard. Pour the oils into a measuring jug and stir them together. With a whisk in one hand and the measuring jug in the other, add the oils to the egg yolks drop by drop, whisking at the same time. Within a minute or two you will notice that the mixture is beginning to thicken. When this happens you can add the oil a little faster, but don't get too confident or it will suddenly curdle because the egg yolks can only absorb the oil at a certain pace.

When you've used half the oil, whisk in 1–2 tablespoons of water to thin it, which will give it a better drizzling consistency

for using on pizzas. Taste and add a little more salt or vinegar if necessary.

You can also make mayonnaise in minutes if you use a food processor. Follow the same method as outlined above.

If the mayonnaise curdles it will suddenly become quite thin, and if left sitting the oil will start to float to the top of the sauce. If this happens you can fix it by putting another egg yolk or 1–2 tablespoons of boiling water into a clean bowl, then whisk in the curdled mayonnaise half a teaspoon at a time until it emulsifies again.

Spoon the mayonnaise into a lidded jar and store in the fridge for up to one week.

Aioli (garlic mayonnaise)

Depending on their size and on how garlicky you want the mayonnaise to be, add 1–4 crushed garlic cloves to the egg yolks at the start of the basic mayonnaise recipe. Add 2 teaspoons of finely chopped fresh flat-leaf parsley at the end and taste for seasoning.

Here's a tip for crushing garlic: put the whole clove of garlic on a chopping board, preferably one that is reserved for garlic and onions. Tap the clove with the flat blade of a kitchen knife to break the skin. Remove the skin and discard it. Sprinkle a few grains of salt onto the clove. Again using the flat blade of the knife, keep pressing the tip of the knife down onto the garlic to form a paste. The salt provides friction so the clove won't shoot off the board.

Or you can use a fine Microplane grater to grate the garlic cloves into a paste. You don't even need to peel the cloves – just start grating them and the papery skins will automatically lift away.

Basil mayonnaise

Pour boiling water over 25 g (1 cup) of fresh basil leaves, count to three, drain and immediately refresh in cold water. Pat the basil dry, then chop and add to the egg yolks when you start to make the basic mayonnaise.

Caper mayonnaise

Place 1 tablespoon of capers on a piece of kitchen paper/paper towel to drain, then stir through the basic mayo.

Chilli basil mayonnaise

Add a good pinch of chilli powder to the egg yolks when making the garlic aioli and add 2 teaspoons of finely chopped basil at the end instead of parsley. Great with salads and sandwiches.

Chipotle chilli mayonnaise

Add 2 tablespoons of crushed chipotle chillies en adobo to the basic mayonnaise.

Coriander/cilantro mayonnaise

Add 1–2 tablespoons of chopped fresh coriander/cilantro to the basic mayonnaise.

Dill mayonnaise

Add 2–3 tablespoons of chopped fresh dill to the mayo.

Fennel mayonnaise

Add 2 tablespoons of finely chopped fennel bulb and 1 tablespoon of Pernod to the basic mayonnaise.

Horseradish mayonnaise

Grate 1–2 teaspoons of fresh horseradish into the basic mayonnaise, depending on how zippy you want it to be. Let it sit for 10 minutes, then taste it and adjust as needed.

Lemon mayonnaise

Use lemon juice instead of white wine vinegar.

Red mustard greens mayonnaise

Finely chop about 10 leaves of red mustard greens or rocket/arugula and stir into the basic mayonnaise.

Roast red pepper mayonnaise

Roast a red pepper (see page 142), place in a bowl and cover with clingfilm/plastic wrap until cool. Peel off the skin and deseed, but keep the juices. Purée the red pepper flesh, then add the purée and juices to the mayo.

Spicy mayonnaise

Add 1–2 teaspoons of Ballymaloe Relish (or a similar tomato-based relish) and ½–1 teaspoon of chilli sauce to the basic recipe.

Tomato mayonnaise

Finely chop three ripe tomatoes, then push them through a fine-mesh sieve and reserve the juices. Use these juices to thin the mayonnaise with instead of water.

Tomato and basil mayonnaise

Add 1–2 tablespoons of a good-quality tomato purée/paste to the basil mayonnaise.

Watercress mayonnaise

Add 4 tablespoons of very finely chopped watercress to the basic mayonnaise.

Wholegrain mustard mayonnaise

Add 1–2 tablespoons of wholegrain mustard to the mayo.

BASIL PESTO

There are three ways to make pesto. You can pound the ingredients separately in a mortar and pestle and then combine them. You can put all the ingredients into a food processor and blend everything together, but you get a much better result when all the ingredients are blitzed separately and then gently stirred together in a mixing bowl. The trick to making pesto in a food processor, though, is not to use one that's too big, otherwise the blade won't catch the ingredients and it will just spin them around instead of chopping them. Or better yet, you could chop everything finely by hand and then stir it all together. Pesto purists swear that it tastes even better when done this way.

50 g (⅓ cup) pine nuts

50 g (⅓ cup) coarsely grated Parmesan, for medium pesto (see method for chunky or fine pesto)

50 g (2 cups) fresh basil leaves

1 garlic clove, crushed or finely chopped

240 ml (1 cup) good-quality extra virgin olive oil

small squeeze of lemon juice

fine sea salt and freshly ground black pepper

Makes 360 ml (1½ cups)

Heat a dry frying pan over a medium heat. When it's hot, add the pine nuts and toast for about 2 minutes, shaking the pan regularly and keeping an eye on them to make sure they don't burn. Once they have a bit of colour and have started to become fragrant, tip them onto a plate and allow to cool. You don't want them to be warm when you combine them with the other ingredients or they could melt the Parmesan.

If you like your pesto to have a chunkier texture, cut a 50 g (1¾ oz) piece of Parmesan into pieces, then pulse in a food processor until it resembles breadcrumbs. If you prefer a smoother pesto, grate the Parmesan more finely on a box grater. Either way, transfer it to a mixing bowl and set aside.

Place the toasted pine nuts in a food processor and pulse until they are ground to the consistency you prefer – you don't want the nuts to be too big. You should aim for the nuts to be the same size as the Parmesan. Transfer to the mixing bowl with the Parmesan.

Place the basil and garlic in the food processor and blitz to a purée, adding some of the olive oil to help it blend if need be. Scrape into the bowl with the Parmesan and pine nuts and stir to combine. Pour in most of the olive oil and mix well, then decide if you need to add the remaining olive oil to get the consistency you like. Season with a squeeze of lemon juice, salt and pepper and give it another stir. Let the pesto sit for 2 minutes to allow the ingredients to marry together, then taste and correct the seasoning with more salt and pepper or another squeeze of lemon juice.

If you're not using the pesto right away, spoon it into a clean jar and top with a thin film of olive oil, which will keep out oxygen and prevent the pesto from turning brown. Store in the fridge for up to two weeks.

VARIATIONS

Wild garlic pesto
Use wild garlic/ramps instead of basil.

Walnut pesto
Use 75 g (¾ cup) walnuts instead of pine nuts and leave out the final squeeze of lemon juice.

SALSA VERDE

Salsa verde is a versatile sauce that tastes good with absolutely everything. My personal favourite is putting salsa verde and aioli together on the same pizza. It's so good!

3 anchovy fillets in oil, drained
1 garlic clove, peeled
2 tbsp capers, drained
zest of 1 lemon
3 tbsp finely chopped fresh
　flat-leaf parsley leaves
1 tbsp finely chopped fresh
　mint leaves

1 tbsp finely chopped rocket/
　arugula
½ tsp fine sea salt
120 ml (½ cup) extra virgin
　olive oil
1 tsp Dijon mustard

Makes 180 ml (¾ cup)

Put the anchovies, garlic and capers in a mortar and pestle and pound into a fine paste. Transfer to a glass or ceramic bowl with the lemon zest, herbs, rocket/arugula and salt and stir to combine, then mix in the olive oil and mustard at the end. Stir well so that all the ingredients come together nicely.

Let the salsa verde sit for about 10 minutes to allow the flavours to marry together, then taste and adjust the seasoning. Store any leftovers in a clean jar in the fridge for up to a week.

GREMOLATA

Gremolata is an Italian condiment that works with literally every pizza and you can use the leftovers to sprinkle on top of pasta or soups. It looks best when everything is chopped very finely and uniformly. Having said that, though, you can leave the parsley a bit bigger than the garlic for a more rustic look. It can also be made in a food processor. You'll get a different result, but it works well if you're making a lot of it.

1 large bunch of fresh
   flat-leaf parsley
1 garlic clove
zest of 1 lemon

Makes 30 g (³/4 cup)

Strip the parsley leaves off the stalks. Make sure they are completely dry before chopping them as finely as you can. Transfer to a bowl.

Chop the garlic as finely as you can, otherwise you might bite on a big bit of raw garlic, which isn't very nice. Transfer to the bowl with the parsley. Add the lemon zest, then mix everything together until well combined. Store any leftovers in an airtight container in the fridge for a day or two.

TZATZIKI

This Greek sauce is usually served with grilled meats or as a cooling dip, but it also works really well with roast lamb on a pizza, like the one on page 103.

½ cucumber
250 g (1 cup) plain Greek yogurt
1 garlic clove, crushed
1 small bunch of fresh mint, flat-leaf parsley or dill, finely chopped
juice of ½ lemon

1 tbsp olive oil
1 tbsp single/light cream
fine sea salt and freshly ground black pepper

Makes 400 g (1½ cups)

Peel the cucumber, cut it in half lengthways and scrape out the seeds with a small spoon, then chop into very, very small dice – about the size of a peppercorn. Place in a bowl and mix together with the rest of the ingredients. Let the dip sit for a few minutes to allow the flavours to marry together, then taste and correct the seasoning. Store any leftovers in an airtight container in the fridge for up to three days.

TAPENADE

This can be a paste or a sauce, depending on how you like it or want to use it. If you add just enough olive oil to bring it all together, then it will be a strong, gutsy paste. If you add more olive oil, then it will be a sauce that's easy to add to a pizza. Sometimes we use a pastry brush to smear lots of tapenade onto the pizza when it comes out of the oven, but it's also good served with crudités, bruschetta or crostini, as a sandwich spread or with lamb, pasta or goats' cheese.

3 anchovy fillets in oil, drained
100 g (1 cup) pitted black olives, finely chopped
1 tsp capers
1 tsp Dijon mustard
splash of olive oil

squeeze of lemon juice
freshly ground black pepper
a little chopped fresh flat-leaf parsley or basil (optional)

Makes 120 ml (½ cup)

Chop the anchovies or pound them in a mortar and pestle until they become a paste, then place in a bowl with the rest of the ingredients and gently mix together until well combined. Let the flavours marry together for a few minutes, then taste and adjust the seasoning. Store any leftovers in a jar in the fridge for up to a week.

PICKLED RED ONIONS

This is a quick pickle that takes only minutes to make. Use it to jazz up pizzas, tacos, quesadillas, fajitas, burgers, salads and braised beef or lamb.

3 red onions
200 ml (¾ cup + 4 tsp) chicken stock or water
60 ml (¼ cup) red wine
60 ml (¼ cup) red wine vinegar
2–3 bay leaves
1 tsp fine sea salt
1 tsp honey or sugar

Makes 500 g (2 cups)

The onions look best when they are thinly sliced as whole rings rather than cut in half. If you leave the hairy root intact on the peeled onions, it makes it easier and safer to slice them on a mandoline. If you don't have a mandoline, then cut the onions in half and slice them thinly with the slicing attachment of a food processor or with a sharp knife. If slicing by hand, cut them lengthways, with the grain of the onion, to get more evenly sized slices. Place the sliced onions in a heatproof glass bowl (don't use a plastic bowl).

Put the remaining ingredients in a saucepan and bring to the boil, then immediately pour the hot liquid over the onions in the bowl. Cover tightly with clingfilm/plastic wrap and put in the fridge for 2 hours, at which point the onions will be bright pink and crisp. Store in a clean jar, covered with the liquid, for up to one month in the fridge. Drain the onions before using them on a pizza.

CARAMELIZED ONIONS

When caramelizing onions, the main ingredient is time – there's no rushing this process, although some people add a pinch of sugar to speed things up. Start cooking the onions well in advance (they keep for days in the fridge) or while you're preheating the oven and getting all the other bits and pieces ready for your pizza.

2 tbsp olive oil
3 large onions, thinly sliced
2 bay leaves
fine sea salt and freshly ground black pepper

Makes 250 g (1 cup)

Heat the olive oil in a saucepan set over a low heat. Add the onions and bay leaves and season generously with salt and pepper. Cook for 20–30 minutes, stirring constantly. You want the onions to stick a bit on the bottom of the saucepan, then scrape them up with a wooden spoon along with any browned bits from the bottom of the pan. Pay attention, though – you don't want them to burn. Once the onions are soft and golden brown, they're ready to use. Store any leftovers in the fridge for up to four days in an airtight container. Alternatively, these also freeze well for up to three months, so you might want to make a double batch, then freeze the rest for another day.

RED ONION JAM

This jam makes pizza taste sweet and succulent. Smear a spoonful directly onto the stretched dough, then hide it with tomato sauce – people who have a pizza with this jam on it will wonder why the pizza tastes so good. Red onion jam is also fantastic with steak sandwiches and burgers.

Unlike most other red onion jam recipes, mine doesn't include any sugar because I don't want it to be too sweet for adding to a pizza, plus the caramelized onions are naturally sweet anyway. A handy thing about this recipe is that it uses 180 ml (¾ cup) of red wine, which is the amount in one of those small single-portion bottles.

2 tbsp olive oil
3 large red onions, halved
    and thinly sliced
2 bay leaves
fine sea salt and freshly
    ground black pepper
180 ml (¾ cup) red wine
1 tsp balsamic vinegar

Makes 250 g (1 cup)

Heat the olive oil in a large frying pan set over a medium–low heat. Add the onions and bay leaves and season generously with salt and pepper. Cook for 20–30 minutes, stirring now and then, until the onions are completely soft and caramelized. You want the onions to stick a bit on the bottom of the saucepan, then scrape them up with a wooden spoon. Pay attention, though – you don't want them to burn.

Stir in the wine and vinegar and bring to the boil, then immediately reduce the heat to low again and simmer for 25–30 minutes more, until almost all the liquid is gone and the onions are meltingly soft and have almost broken down into a jammy consistency that you can practically smear onto the pizza dough. Transfer to a clean jar and store in the fridge for up to three months.

PEPERONATA

You can use peperonata as a topping for pizza, but also as a sauce for pasta, a side for grilled fish or meat, as a filling for omelettes or a frittata or served on top of polenta or mashed potatoes. It even works in sandwiches. It's good hot, cold or at room temperature and it freezes well in small tubs. It's so versatile that you might want to make a double batch so that you always have some on hand in the freezer for those days when there's nothing else in the fridge or cupboard.

2 tbsp olive oil
1 garlic clove, crushed
1 onion, sliced
2 red bell peppers
2 green bell peppers
6 large, ripe tomatoes
fine sea salt and freshly
    ground black pepper
pinch of sugar
a few leaves of fresh basil
    (optional)

Makes 750 g (3 cups)

Warm the olive oil in a flameproof heavy-bottomed casserole/Dutch oven set over a medium–low heat. Add the garlic and cook for a few seconds. Add the sliced onion, toss it in the oil and allow to soften, covered, while you prepare the peppers.

Halve the peppers and remove the seeds, then cut the peppers into quarters and cut again into 2.5 cm (1 in) squares. Add to the casserole/Dutch oven with the onion, replace the lid and continue to cook.

Meanwhile, scald the tomatoes in boiling water for 10 seconds, pour off the water and peel them immediately. Slice the tomatoes and add to the casserole/Dutch oven. Season with salt, freshly ground pepper, a pinch of sugar and a few leaves of fresh basil, if using. Cook for about 30 minutes, uncovered, until the vegetables are soft and have formed a thick stew. If you're using the peperonata as a pizza topping, continue to simmer it until most of the liquid has cooked away. Store any leftovers in an airtight container in the fridge for up to three days or freeze in small tubs for up to three months.

TOMATO SALSA

Salsa works surprisingly well on a pizza. If you want a spicy salsa, add the fresh chilli. If not, just leave it out. You can also use any herb you like instead of coriander/cilantro or basil – try parsley, marjoram or even tarragon.

3 ripe tomatoes, finely
    chopped
½ red onion, finely
    chopped
½ fresh red or green chilli,
    deseeded and finely
    chopped (optional)
squeeze of lime juice
1 tbsp olive oil

1 tbsp roughly chopped
    fresh coriander/cilantro
    or basil leaves
fine sea salt and freshly
    ground black pepper

Makes 500 g (2 cups)

Gently combine all the ingredients in a bowl. Let the salsa sit for at least 5 minutes to allow the flavours to marry together, then taste and adjust the seasoning. Strain the salsa before using it on a pizza, as the tomatoes will release their juices as the salsa sits. Store any leftovers in an airtight container in the fridge for up to three days.

GUACAMOLE

Guacamole works just as well as a dip for pizza crusts as it does for tortilla chips. Try it, you'll see!

1 ripe avocado
1 garlic clove, crushed
1–2 tbsp freshly squeezed
    lemon or lime juice
1 tbsp chopped fresh
    coriander/cilantro, basil
    or parsley
fine sea salt and freshly
    ground black pepper

Makes 125 g (½ cup)

Cut the avocado in half, remove the stone and scoop the flesh into a bowl. Mash with a fork, then add all the other ingredients and mix gently. Taste and correct the seasoning with a little more lemon or lime juice and salt or pepper if necessary.

This is best served immediately. Otherwise, cover the surface of the guacamole with a sheet of clingfilm/plastic wrap to keep out the air, which is what will turn it brown, and keep in the fridge for up to a few hours.

CHILLI OIL

We make this with fresh chillies when they're available from our glasshouses or dried chilli/hot red pepper flakes when they're not. If you make it with the flakes, it will turn the oil a fiery orange colour. Chilli oil can be drizzled over all sorts of pizzas, but you could also use it to liven up a steak, grilled chicken or fish or even popcorn. Or try cooking with it instead of your regular olive oil to add a kick to whatever dish you're making.

240 ml (1 cup) good-quality extra virgin olive oil

1 medium-sized fresh red chilli, deseeded and finely chopped, or 1 tsp dried chilli/hot red pepper flakes

Makes 240 ml (1 cup)

Put the oil and chopped chilli or dried chilli/hot red pepper flakes into a small saucepan. Heat gently over a low heat until the oil is just warmed through, then remove from the heat and allow to cool completely. Be careful not to burn the oil, which can easily happen. Pour the oil into a measuring jug to make it easier to then pour into a clean jar. Seal the jar and store the chilli oil in the fridge for up to one month. It might turn cloudy from the cold, but bring it back to room temperature before you want to use it and it will clear up again.

POUNDED PARSLEY AND GARLIC OIL

When using a mortar and pestle, don't be afraid to make a lot of noise! The more you pound the parsley, garlic and chilli, the better the oil will taste because it means you're really crushing the plant cells and releasing more of the volatile aromatics than you would if you just chop them. A top tip when making this oil is to visualize drizzling it onto the pizza. When you add the oil you can then regulate it to get the consistency you want.

4–6 heaped tbsp chopped fresh flat-leaf parsley
1 small garlic clove, peeled
½ tsp finely diced fresh chilli or dried chilli/ hot red pepper flakes (optional)
pinch of fine sea salt
120–180 ml (½–¾ cup) good-quality olive oil

Makes 125–180 ml (½–¾ cup)

Put the parsley, garlic, chilli (if using) and a pinch of salt in a mortar and pestle. Pound together really, really well, until it forms a paste, then pound some more for good measure before mixing in 120 ml (½ cup) of the olive oil.

Check the consistency at this point and decide whether you want to add some or all of the remaining oil (see the note above). Pour the oil into a measuring jug to make it easier to then pour into a clean jar. Seal the jar and store the oil in the fridge for up to one month. It might eventually turn cloudy from the cold, but bring it back to room temperature before you want to use it and it will clear up again.

TOFFEE SAUCE

This irresistible sauce is delicious served with ice cream or drizzled over pancakes for a decadent breakfast, but it's even better with sliced bananas. It's also an essential part of the banoffee pizza on page 187. It keeps for weeks in the fridge, so I'm sure you'll find plenty of uses for it.

300 g (1 cup) golden syrup
100 g (4 oz/1 stick) butter
150 g (¾ cup) soft dark brown sugar
75 g (⅓ cup) granulated sugar
240 ml (1 cup) single/light cream
½ tsp vanilla extract

Makes 600 ml (2½ cups)

Put the golden syrup, butter and sugars in a heavy-bottomed saucepan. Stir as it melts gently on a low heat. Simmer for 4–5 minutes, then remove from the heat and gradually stir in the cream and vanilla extract. Put back on a low heat and stir constantly for a further 2–3 minutes, until the sauce is absolutely smooth.

The toffee sauce will keep for several weeks stored in a sealed jar in the fridge. It can be served either warm, hot or cold.

SAUSAGE PIZZAS

Don't be put off by the idea of making homemade sausage. You aren't putting any of these sausages into a casing, so they are actually really simple to make. The key is to use good-quality meat with a nice amount of fat – a good ratio is 70 per cent lean meat, 30 per cent fat.

There are two ways of making the sausage meat. If your meat is already minced (you can ask your butcher to do this for you), just mix all the ingredients together in a mixing bowl. The second way is to mince the meat yourself. Cut the meat into small pieces and place it in a bowl with the other ingredients, mixing well to combine, then push it through a mincer. This will give a different texture and a better flavour, but either way is perfectly good.

All these sausage recipes make 450 g (1 lb) and will keep for up to three days in the fridge. If you have leftovers, sausage meat freezes well for up to six months.

BALLYMALOE SAUSAGE

450 g (1 lb) minced/ground pork
60 g (1 cup) fresh white
    breadcrumbs
1 garlic clove, crushed
1 egg, lightly beaten
2 tbsp finely chopped mixed fresh
    herbs, such as parsley, thyme,
    chives, marjoram, rosemary
    and sage

1 tsp fine sea salt
freshly ground black pepper
olive oil, for frying

Mix together all the ingredients except the olive oil in a large bowl. Heat a little olive oil in a pan and fry off a knob of the sausage meat to make sure the seasoning is correct. Adjust if necessary.

FENNEL SAUSAGE

1 heaped tbsp fennel seeds
450 g (1 lb) minced/ground pork
1 garlic clove, crushed
1 tsp fine sea salt
freshly ground black pepper
olive oil, for frying

Toast the fennel seeds to release their flavour: put them into a dry frying pan and toast them on a high heat for about 2 minutes, shaking the pan now and then, until they start to pop. Using a mortar and pestle, spice grinder or even a coffee grinder, pound or blend the seeds to a fine powder.

Mix together all the ingredients except the olive oil in a large bowl. Heat a little olive oil in a pan and fry off a knob of the sausage meat to make sure the seasoning is correct. Adjust if necessary.

SPICY SAUSAGE

450 g (1 lb) minced/ground pork
1 garlic clove, crushed
1 tsp paprika (smoked, sweet or hot)
1 tsp fine sea salt

½–1 tsp chilli powder or cayenne
    pepper, according to taste
½ tsp freshly ground black pepper
dash of olive oil

Mix together all the ingredients in a large bowl. Heat a little olive oil in a pan and fry off a knob of the sausage meat to make sure the seasoning is correct. Adjust if necessary.

ROSÉ VEAL SAUSAGE

450 g (1 lb) minced/ground
    rosé veal
1 garlic clove, crushed
2 tbsp olive oil, plus extra
    for frying

2 tbsp finely chopped fresh sage
1 tsp fine sea salt
freshly ground black pepper

Mix all the ingredients in a large bowl. Heat a little olive oil in a pan and fry off a knob of the sausage meat to test the seasoning. Adjust if necessary.

SIMPLE LAMB SAUSAGE

You can use spring lamb, regular lamb or mutton for this mince, depending on what's available or what you prefer. Meat from the leg or shoulder is also good and is a little less expensive too. The main thing is that the mince should contain a good bit of fat (the white bits flecked throughout the mince), which makes a big difference to the flavour. If your mince doesn't have much fat, add a bit of butter or olive oil.

450 g (1 lb) minced/ground lamb
1 garlic clove, crushed
1 tsp fine sea salt
freshly ground black pepper
olive oil, for frying

Mix together all the ingredients except the olive oil in a large bowl. Heat a little olive oil in a pan and fry off a knob of the sausage meat to make sure the seasoning is correct. Adjust if necessary.

MOROCCAN LAMB SAUSAGE

1 tsp cumin seeds
1 tsp coriander seeds
1 tsp fennel seeds
450 g (1 lb) minced/ground lamb
1 garlic clove, crushed
1 tsp fine sea salt
freshly ground black pepper
olive oil, for frying

Toasting the seeds helps to release their flavour, so put them into a dry frying pan and toast them on a high heat for about 2 minutes, shaking the pan now and then, until they start to pop. Using a mortar and pestle, a spice grinder or even a coffee grinder, pound or blend the seeds to a fine powder.

Mix together all the ingredients except the olive oil in a large bowl. Heat a little olive oil in a pan and fry off a knob of the sausage meat to make sure the seasoning is correct. Adjust if necessary.

MEATBALL VARIATIONS

Try these variations if making the meatball pizza on page 80.

• Salt, pepper, crushed garlic, chopped fresh parsley and a dash of olive oil is an easy option that works with minced/ground beef, lamb, pork and even chicken. I think beef meatballs taste the best when prepared this way.

• A mixture of half beef, half pork is also a good option. In this case, add 1 tablespoon of finely chopped fresh thyme and/or tarragon.

• Pork works well with toasted and ground fennel, cumin and coriander seeds. Add 1 teaspoon of each for 450 g (1 lb) of meat along with one crushed garlic clove and some salt and pepper.

• If you have any meat mixture left over – or if you want to make extra expressly for this purpose – form them into slightly larger balls or patties and serve them as sliders with the leftover wholegrain mustard mayonnaise.

BEEF WITH BÉARNAISE SAUCE

To make this pizza especially sensational, use the best beef you can, preferably dry-aged beef or meat from a special breed such as Angus, Herefordshire or even Kobe if you want to go really high end. You don't have to use the fillet or sirloin, the priciest cuts. Other parts from the leg are more affordable and perfect for mincing/grinding.

2 balls of pizza dough
    (pages 26–35)
pinch of fine sea salt
1 tbsp olive oil
160 ml (²⁄₃ cup) tomato
    sauce (page 44)
250 g (2 cups) grated
    mozzarella
225 g (1 cup) lean minced/
    ground beef
pinch of flaky sea salt,
    such as Maldon
4 tbsp Béarnaise sauce
    (page 48)
1 sprig of fresh tarragon,
    to garnish

*Makes 2 x 25 cm
(10 in) pizzas*

Preheat the oven to 250°C/480°F/gas mark 9 or as high as it will go. Place a pizza stone or an upside-down baking tray in the oven to heat up too. Get all your ingredients and equipment ready, including taking the dough out of the fridge 1 hour before you're ready to cook.

Stretch the pizza dough by hand or roll it out as per the instructions on pages 24–25. Sprinkle a pinch of salt evenly over the dough, then brush a little olive oil onto the rim with a pastry brush to help it turn golden.

Using a ladle or big spoon, pour the tomato sauce in the centre of the dough. Spread the sauce over the pizza in concentric circles with the back of the ladle or spoon, leaving a 2.5 cm (1 in) border clear around the edges for the crust. You only want a thin layer of sauce.

Place a big handful of the grated mozzarella in a mound in the middle of the dough. Use your palm to spread it out evenly across the pizza, leaving the edges clear for the crust.

Check that there is no liquid on the peel or board or your pizza won't slide off it. Shake the board gently to see if the pizza will move. If it doesn't, lift up the pizza with a dough cutter or spatula and sprinkle a little flour on the board until it does move easily.

Shape the beef into little balls the size of a coin and add it to the pizza, aiming to get a good balance of beef across the pizza. We find that the beef tastes best when it's still a little pink in the middle and add it halfway through cooking, but if you like your beef more well done, add it at the start.

Slide the pizza off the peel or board onto the pizza stone or upside-down baking tray in the hot oven. Cook for 7–10 minutes, but start checking it after 5 minutes – you want the bottom and the crust to be cooked through and golden and the cheese should be melted.

Take the pizza out of the oven and transfer to a wire cooling rack, then sprinkle the beef with a pinch of flaky sea salt, drizzle over the Béarnaise sauce and scatter over the tarragon. Allow to stand for 1 minute before cutting into slices.

BALLYMALOE SAUSAGE WITH ROCKET AND RED PEPPER MAYONNAISE

At the cookery school, we call this meat Mrs Allen's sausage. Myrtle Allen is the grande dame of Irish cooking. She has influenced thousands of kitchens in Ireland and beyond and has paved the way for her children, grandchildren and many other family members to succeed in various food companies – including Saturday Pizzas. This is the sausage recipe that Myrtle has been using at Ballymaloe House for 50 years.

2 handfuls of rocket/arugula
2 tbsp olive oil
pinch of fine sea salt
2 balls of pizza dough (pages 26–35)
160 ml (²/₃ cup) tomato sauce (page 44)
250 g (2 cups) grated mozzarella
200 g (³/₄ cup) Ballymaloe sausage meat (page 64)
2–4 tbsp roast red pepper mayonnaise (page 51)

Makes enough for 2 x 25 cm (10 in) pizzas

Preheat the oven to 250°C/480°F/gas mark 9 or as high as it will go. Place a pizza stone or an upside-down baking tray in the oven to heat up too. Get all your ingredients and equipment ready, including taking the dough out of the fridge 1 hour before you're ready to cook.

Place the rocket/arugula in a bowl. Drizzle with half the olive oil and season with a pinch of salt (no need for pepper). Toss to coat all the leaves with the oil. This adds extra flavour and also helps protect the rocket/arugula from the heat of the oven so that it doesn't burn.

Stretch the pizza dough by hand or roll it out as per the instructions on pages 24–25. Sprinkle a pinch of salt evenly over the dough, then brush the remaining olive oil onto the rim to help it turn golden.

Using a ladle or big spoon, pour the tomato sauce in the centre of the dough. Spread the sauce over the pizza in concentric circles with the back of the ladle or spoon, leaving a 2.5 cm (1 in) border clear around the edges for the crust. You only want a thin layer of sauce.

Place a big handful of the mozzarella in the middle of the dough and spread it evenly, leaving the crust edges clear. Put 8–12 walnut-sized knobs of the raw sausage meat on top, spreading them evenly across the pizza. If the pieces are too small, the meat will overcook.

Check that there is no liquid on the peel or board or your pizza won't slide off it. Shake the board gently to see if the pizza will move. If it doesn't, lift up the pizza with a dough cutter or spatula and sprinkle a little flour on the board until it does move easily.

Slide the pizza off the peel or board onto the pizza stone or upside-down baking tray in the hot oven. Cook for 7–10 minutes, but start checking it after 5 minutes – you want the bottom and the crust to be cooked through and golden and the cheese should be melted.

Take the pizza out of the oven and scatter over the rocket/arugula. Return it to the oven for 30 seconds–1 minute, until the rocket/arugula just starts to wilt. Alternatively, skip this step and keep the leaves fresh, letting them wilt only slightly in the residual heat of the pizza.

Transfer to a wire cooling rack, then drizzle with the red pepper mayonnaise. Allow to stand for 1 minute before slicing.

FENNEL SAUSAGE WITH SALSA VERDE

We have a really nice customer from Dublin who absolutely adores this pizza. One day he sent us a message to say that he would be in Cork in three weeks' time and asked if we could put his favourite pizza on the menu that week. We said no problem, but totally forgot! After the menu went up online, it took him 30 seconds to respond: 'Hey, what happened to the fennel sausage and salsa verde pizza? I'm driving three hours for that pizza!' I had to apologize profusely, explaining again about how much prep is involved.

But on Saturday morning the prep went really well, so I went ahead and put the fennel sausage and salsa verde pizza on the menu, too. Our Dublin friend and his family came in as soon as our doors opened at 12:30, happy to be at the Ballymaloe Cookery School but also slightly disappointed because we weren't serving his favourite pizza. But as he looked at the board and saw it there after all, his face lit up. The kids started cheering when they heard the news and his wife just rolled her eyes in relief.

2 balls of pizza dough
　　(pages 26–35)
pinch of fine sea salt
1 tbsp olive oil
160 ml (²⁄₃ cup) tomato
　　sauce (page 44)
250 g (2 cups) grated
　　mozzarella
200 g (1 cup) fennel
　　sausage meat (page 64)
4 tbsp salsa verde
　　(page 53)

*Makes enough for
2 x 25 cm (10 in)
pizzas*

Preheat the oven to 250°C/480°F/gas mark 9 or as high as it will go. Place a pizza stone or an upside-down baking tray in the oven to heat up too. Get all your ingredients and equipment ready, including taking the dough out of the fridge 1 hour before you're ready to cook.

Stretch the pizza dough by hand or roll it out as per the instructions on pages 24–25. Sprinkle a pinch of salt evenly over the dough, then brush a little olive oil onto the rim with a pastry brush to help it turn golden.

Using a ladle or big spoon, pour the tomato sauce in the centre of the dough. Spread the sauce over the pizza in concentric circles with the back of the ladle or spoon, leaving a 2.5 cm (1 in) border clear around the edges for the crust. You only want a thin layer of sauce.

Place a big handful of the mozzarella in a mound in the middle of the dough and spread it evenly, leaving the crust edges

clear. Put 8–12 walnut-sized knobs of the raw sausage meat on top, spreading them evenly across the pizza. If the pieces are too small, the meat will overcook.

Check that there is no liquid on the peel or board or your pizza won't slide off it. Shake the board gently to see if the pizza will move. If it doesn't, lift up the pizza with a dough cutter or spatula and sprinkle a little flour on the board until it does move easily.

Slide the pizza off the peel or board onto the pizza stone or upside-down baking tray in the hot oven. Cook for 7–10 minutes, but start checking it after 5 minutes – you want the bottom and the crust to be cooked through and golden and the cheese should be melted.

Take the pizza out of the oven, then drizzle with the salsa verde. Allow to stand for 1 minute before slicing to serve.

VARIATIONS

Instead of adding salsa verde at the end, this fennel sausage pizza also works well with aioli (page 51) and some fresh thyme leaves, basil or wild garlic pesto (page 52) or roast red pepper mayonnaise (page 51).

ROSÉ VEAL SAUSAGE WITH ROAST PEPPERS AND FENNEL MAYONNAISE

Rosé veal is a decadent treat that we put on the menu every now and then. Veal is the meat from a calf that is usually less than eight months old. There are different farming systems for veal and some are more controversial than others. Some calves are kept indoors and fed milk, milk powder and additional foods, resulting in tender, pale white meat. This system is popular in countries like France, Germany, Italy and the Netherlands. Another system is to keep the calf in the field with its mother and separate them only at night. This results in meat that is more pink than white – hence the name rosé veal. This method is seen as more ethical and it's the way we raise our veal calves at the Ballymaloe Cookery School.

1 red bell pepper

1 yellow bell pepper

1 tbsp olive oil

2 balls of pizza dough (pages 26–35)

160 ml (2/3 cup) tomato sauce (page 44)

250 g (2 cups) grated mozzarella

200 g (1 cup) rosé veal sausage meat (page 64)

2–4 tbsp fennel mayonnaise (page 51)

fine sea salt and freshly ground black pepper

Makes 2 x 25 cm (10 in) pizzas

Preheat the oven to 250°C/480°F/gas mark 9 or as high as it will go. Line a baking tray with foil.

Place the whole bell peppers on the lined tray and roast in the hot oven for 30–40 minutes, turning once or twice, until the skins are blackened all over. Remove from the oven and seal them in the foil to steam them and make them easier to peel. After about 30 minutes, peel the peppers and remove the stems and seeds. Cut into thick strips, then cut each strip in half widthways. Set aside.

Once the peppers come out of the oven, place a pizza stone or an upside-down baking tray in the oven to heat up. Get all your ingredients and equipment ready, including taking the dough out of the fridge 1 hour before you're ready to cook.

Stretch the pizza dough by hand or roll it out as per the instructions on pages 24–25. Sprinkle a pinch of salt evenly over the dough, then brush a little olive oil onto the rim to help it turn golden. Using a ladle or big spoon, pour the tomato sauce in the centre of the dough. Spread the sauce in concentric

circles with the back of the ladle or spoon, leaving a 2.5 cm (1 in) border clear around the edges. You want a thin layer of sauce.

Place a big handful of the mozzarella in the middle of the pizza and spread it evenly, leaving the crust edges clear. Scatter the peppers on top of the cheese along with 8–12 walnut-sized knobs of the raw sausage meat, spreading them evenly across the pizza. If the pieces are too small, the meat will overcook.

Check that there is no liquid on the peel or board or your pizza won't slide off it. If the pizza doesn't move when you shake the board gently, lift it up with a dough cutter or spatula and sprinkle a little flour on the board until it does move easily. Slide the pizza off the peel or board onto the pizza stone or upside-down baking tray in the hot oven. Cook for 7–10 minutes, but start checking it after 5 minutes – you want the bottom and the crust to be cooked through and golden and the cheese should be melted.

Take the pizza out of the oven, transfer to a cooling rack, then drizzle the fennel mayo over. Stand for 1 minute, then cut in slices.

LAMB SAUSAGE WITH MINT AND AIOLI

There are two lamb sausage recipes on page 65: one for Moroccan lamb sausage, seasoned with cumin, coriander and fennel seeds, and one for a simple lamb sausage with just garlic, salt and pepper. Either one will work well with the combination of fresh mint and aioli on this pizza.

1 tbsp olive oil

2 balls of pizza dough (pages 26–35)

pinch of fine sea salt

160 ml (2/3 cup) tomato sauce (page 44)

250 g (2 cups) grated mozzarella

200 g (1 cup) simple lamb or Moroccan lamb sausage meat (page 65)

1 tbsp roughly chopped fresh mint

2–4 tbsp aioli (page 51)

Makes 2 x 25 cm (10 in) pizzas

Preheat the oven to 250°C/480°F/gas mark 9 or as high as it will go. Place a pizza stone or an upside-down baking tray in the oven to heat up too. Get all your ingredients and equipment ready, including taking the dough out of the fridge 1 hour before you're ready to cook.

Stretch the pizza dough by hand or roll it out as per the instructions on pages 24–25. Sprinkle a pinch of salt evenly over the dough, then brush a little olive oil onto the rim with a pastry brush to help it turn golden.

Using a ladle or big spoon, pour the tomato sauce in the centre of the dough. Spread the sauce over the pizza in concentric circles with the back of the ladle or spoon, leaving a 2.5 cm (1 in) border clear around the edges for the crust. You only want a thin layer of sauce.

Place a big handful of the mozzarella in a mound in the middle of the pizza and spread it evenly, leaving the crust edges clear. Put 8–12 walnut-sized knobs of the raw sausage meat on top, spreading them evenly across the pizza. If the pieces are too small, the meat will overcook.

Check that there is no liquid on the peel or board or your pizza won't slide off it. Shake the board gently to see if the pizza will move. If it doesn't, lift up the pizza with a dough cutter or spatula and sprinkle a little flour on the board until it does move easily.

Slide the pizza off the peel or board onto the pizza stone or upside-down baking tray in the hot oven. Cook for 7–10 minutes, but start checking it after 5 minutes – you want the bottom and the crust to be cooked through and golden and the cheese should be melted.

Take the pizza out of the oven and transfer to a wire cooling rack, then scatter over the fresh mint and drizzle with aioli. Allow to stand for 1 minute before cutting into slices.

VARIATION

Lamb sausage with Parmesan, tapenade & aioli

Make the pizzas as per the recipe above, but when they come out of the oven, scatter over a generous amount of freshly grated Parmesan, dot with spoonfuls of tapenade (page 55) and drizzle with 2–4 tablespoons of aioli.

Use the simple lamb sausage for this variation since there are so many gutsy flavours, from the Parmesan and tapenade to the aioli.

SAUSAGE WITH GOATS' CHEESE AND CARAMELIZED ONIONS

This is an unfussy but flavour-packed combination that works well with any of the sausage recipes on pages 64–65, so go ahead and use your favourite kind.

2 balls of pizza dough
    (pages 26–35)
pinch of fine sea salt
1 tbsp olive oil
160 ml (²⁄₃ cup) tomato
    sauce (page 44)
250 g (2 cups) grated
    mozzarella
150 g (½ cup) caramelized
    onions (page 56)
200 g (1 cup) sausage
    meat (see recipe
    introduction)
80 g (⅓ cup) soft goats'
    cheese, preferably
    Ardsallagh or St Tola

*Makes 2 x 25 cm
(10 in) pizzas*

Preheat the oven to 250°C/480°F/gas mark 9 or as high as it will go. Place a pizza stone or an upside-down baking tray in the oven to heat up too. Get all your ingredients and equipment ready, including taking the dough out of the fridge 1 hour before you're ready to cook.

Stretch each pizza dough ball by hand or roll it out as per the instructions on pages 24–25. Sprinkle a pinch of salt evenly over the dough, then brush a little olive oil onto the rim with a pastry brush to help it turn golden.

Using a ladle or big spoon, pour the tomato sauce in the centre of the dough. Spread the sauce over the pizza in concentric circles with the back of the ladle or spoon, leaving a 2.5 cm (1 in) border clear around the edges for the crust. You only want a thin layer of sauce.

Place a big handful of the mozzarella in a mound in the middle of the dough and spread it evenly, leaving the crust edges clear. Scatter over the caramelized onions, then put 8–12 walnut-sized knobs of

the raw sausage meat on top, spreading them evenly across the pizza. If the pieces are too small, the meat will overcook.

Dot small knobs (about ½ teaspoon each) of the goats' cheese between the meat, aiming to get a good balance of ingredients across the pizza.

Check that there is no liquid on the peel or board or your pizza won't slide off it. Shake the board gently to see if the pizza will move. If it doesn't, lift up the pizza with a dough cutter or spatula and sprinkle a little flour on the board until it does move easily.

Slide the pizza off the peel or board onto the pizza stone or upside-down baking tray in the hot oven. Cook for 7–10 minutes, but start checking it after 5 minutes – you want the bottom and the crust to be cooked through and golden and the cheese should be melted.

Take the pizza out of the oven and transfer to a wire cooling rack. Allow to stand for 1 minute before cutting into slices.

SPICY SAUSAGE WITH BÉCHAMEL, PECORINO, TAPENADE AND GREMOLATA

All the different elements of this pizza require a lot of prep, but the extra effort is well worth it when you want to push the boat out a little. If you are short of time, you could always use the tomato sauce on page 44 instead of the béchamel and choose just the tapenade or just the gremolata, depending on whether you want the salty hit from the tapenade or a fresh burst of flavour from the herby gremolata.

2 balls of pizza dough
    (pages 26–35)
pinch of fine sea salt
1 tbsp olive oil
8–10 tbsp béchamel sauce
    (page 46)
250 g (2 cups) grated
    mozzarella
200 g (1 cup) spicy
    sausage meat (page 64)
1 tbsp finely grated
    Pecorino cheese
2–4 tbsp tapenade
    (page 55)
2–4 tbsp gremolata
    (page 54)

*Makes 2 x 25 cm
(10 in) pizzas*

Preheat the oven to 250°C/480°F/gas mark 9 or as high as it will go. Place a pizza stone or an upside-down baking tray in the oven to heat up too. Get all your ingredients and equipment ready, including taking the dough out of the fridge 1 hour before you're ready to cook.

Stretch the pizza dough by hand or roll it out as per the instructions on pages 24–25. Sprinkle a pinch of salt evenly over the dough. Brush a very thin rim of crust with oil on each one to help it turn golden. You don't want to brush on too much because the béchamel will slide off it when you try to spread it over the dough later on.

Using a ladle or big spoon, pour 4–5 tablespoons of béchamel in the centre of the dough. Spread the sauce over the pizza in concentric circles with the back of the ladle or spoon, leaving a 2.5 cm (1 in) border clear around the edges for the crust.

Place a big handful of the mozzarella in a mound in the middle of the dough and spread it evenly, leaving the crust edges clear. Crumble the raw sausage meat on top, spreading it evenly across the pizza.

Check that there is no liquid on the peel or board or your pizza won't slide off it. Shake the board gently to see if the pizza will move. If it doesn't, lift up the pizza with a dough cutter or spatula and sprinkle a little flour on the board until it does move easily.

Slide the pizza off the peel or board onto the pizza stone or upside-down baking tray in the hot oven. Cook for 7–10 minutes, but start checking it after 5 minutes – you want the bottom and the crust to be cooked through and golden and the cheese should be melted.

Take the pizza out of the oven and transfer to a wire cooling rack. Sprinkle over the Pecorino cheese, then dollop the tapenade all over the pizza and sprinkle generously with the gremolata. Allow to stand for 1 minute before slicing.

MEATBALLS WITH BLACK OLIVES, PARMESAN AND WHOLEGRAIN MUSTARD MAYONNAISE

This one is for meat lovers, but don't be tempted to add more than three or four meatballs per pizza or it will be way too much meat. Check out the variations on page 65 too.

400 g (2 cups) minced/ground beef

1 garlic clove, crushed

1 tbsp finely chopped fresh flat-leaf parsley, plus extra to garnish

2 tbsp olive oil

2 balls of pizza dough (pages 26–35)

160 ml (2/3 cup) tomato sauce (page 44)

250 g (2 cups) grated mozzarella

10–12 black olives, pitted and halved

2–4 tbsp finely grated Parmesan

2–4 tbsp wholegrain mustard mayonnaise (page 51)

fine sea salt and freshly ground black pepper

Makes 2 x 25 cm (10 in) pizzas

Preheat the oven to 200°C/400°F/gas mark 6. Line a baking tray with tin foil.

Place the beef in a mixing bowl with the crushed garlic, chopped parsley, half of the olive oil and some salt and pepper. Mix together until well combined. Use an ice cream scoop to make six to eight same-sized meatballs and place on the lined tray. Bake in the oven for 10 minutes to make sure they'll be fully cooked through after their second blast in the oven on top of the pizzas later on. Allow to cool slightly, then cut each meatball in half.

When the meatballs come out of the oven, raise the temperature to 250°C/480°F/gas mark 9 or as high as it will go. Place a pizza stone or an upside-down baking tray in the oven to heat up too. Get all your ingredients and equipment ready, including taking the dough out of the fridge 1 hour before you're ready to cook.

Stretch the pizza dough by hand or roll it out as per the instructions on pages 24–25. Sprinkle a pinch of salt evenly over the dough, then brush a little olive oil onto the rim with a pastry brush to help it turn golden.

Using a ladle or big spoon, pour the tomato sauce in the centre of the dough. Spread the sauce over the pizza in concentric circles with the back of the ladle or spoon, leaving a 2.5 cm (1 in) border clear around the edges for the crust. You only want a thin layer of sauce.

Place a big handful of the grated mozzarella in a mound in the middle of the dough. Use your palm to spread it out evenly across the pizza, leaving the edges clear for the crust. Place three to four halved meatballs on top of the cheese and scatter over the halved olives, aiming to get a good balance of ingredients across the pizza.

Check that there is no liquid on the peel or board or your pizza won't slide off it. Shake the board gently to see if the pizza will move. If it doesn't, lift up the pizza with a dough cutter or spatula and sprinkle a little flour on the board until it does move easily.

Slide the pizza off the peel or board onto the pizza stone or upside-down baking tray in the hot oven. Cook for 7–10 minutes, but start checking it after 5 minutes – you want the bottom and the crust to be cooked through and golden and the cheese should be melted.

Take the pizza out of the oven. Scatter over the Parmesan, then drizzle with the wholegrain mustard mayonnaise. Allow to stand for 1 minute before slicing.

CURED MEAT PIZZAS

Italians have a long tradition of curing meat, so it's only natural that cured meats are some of the most popular pizza toppings. They are one of the easiest ways of adding instant flavour.

PEPPERONI

No matter what specials we have on the menu, this is our most popular pizza and it always has been. Have you ever noticed that even the pizza emoji is a pepperoni pizza? People just love it.

2 balls of pizza dough
    (pages 26–35)
3 tbsp finely grated
    Parmesan
1 tbsp finely chopped
    fresh flat-leaf parsley
pinch of fine sea salt
1 tbsp olive oil
160 ml (²⁄₃ cup) tomato
    sauce (page 44)
250 g (2 cups) grated
    mozzarella
16 slices of pepperoni

*Makes 2 x 25 cm
(10 in) pizzas*

Preheat the oven to 250°C/480°F/gas mark 9 or as high as it will go. Place a pizza stone or an upside-down baking tray in the oven to heat up too. Get all your ingredients and equipment ready, including taking the dough out of the fridge 1 hour before you're ready to cook.

Place the grated Parmesan and chopped parsley in a bowl and mix together until well combined.

Stretch the pizza dough by hand or roll it out as per the instructions on pages 24–25. Sprinkle a pinch of salt evenly over the dough, then brush a little olive oil onto the rim with a pastry brush to help it turn golden.

Using a ladle or big spoon, pour the tomato sauce in the centre of the dough. Spread it over the pizza in concentric circles with the back of the ladle or spoon, leaving a 2.5 cm (1 in) border clear around the edges for the crust. You only want a thin layer of sauce.

Place a big handful of the grated mozzarella in a mound in the middle of the dough. Use your palm to spread it out evenly across the pizza, leaving the edges clear for the crust. Scatter the pepperoni on top of the cheese, aiming to get a good balance of ingredients across the pizza.

Check that there is no liquid on the peel or board or your pizza won't slide off it. Shake the board gently to see if the pizza will move. If it doesn't, lift up the pizza with a dough cutter or spatula and sprinkle a little flour on the board until it does move easily.

Slide the pizza off the peel or board onto the pizza stone or upside-down baking tray in the hot oven. Cook for 7–10 minutes, but start checking it after 5 minutes – you want the bottom and the crust to be cooked through and golden and the cheese should be melted.

Take the pizza out of the oven and transfer to a wire cooling rack, then sprinkle over the Parmesan and parsley mixture. Allow to stand for 1 minute before cutting into slices.

ALL-DAY BREAKFAST PIZZA

A special part of Saturday Pizzas is that the cookery school's 12-week students begin and end their time at Ballymaloe with pizza. When they arrive, we make pizzas for them on their first night here during a casual party in the barn so that everyone can get to know each other. And then three months later, the day after their last party when their exams are done, we make them this breakfast pizza before sending them back into the world.

2 balls of pizza dough
   (pages 26–35)
2 handfuls of rocket/
   arugula or wild garlic
2 tbsp olive oil
2 pinches of fine sea salt
160 ml (2/3 cup) tomato
   sauce (page 44)
250 g (2 cups) grated
   mozzarella
2 slices of bacon, cut into
   small dice
2 eggs

*Makes 2 x 25 cm
(10 in) pizzas*

Preheat the oven to 250°C/480°F/gas mark 9 or as high as it will go. Place a pizza stone or an upside-down baking tray in the oven to heat up too. Get all your ingredients and equipment ready, including taking the dough out of the fridge 1 hour before you're ready to cook.

Place the rocket/arugula or wild garlic in a bowl. Drizzle with half of the oil and season with a pinch of salt. Toss to combine and coat all the leaves. This adds flavour and helps protect the greens from burning.

Stretch the pizza dough by hand or roll it out as per the instructions on pages 24–25. Sprinkle a pinch of salt evenly over the dough, then brush a little oil onto the rim to help it turn golden.

Using a ladle or big spoon, pour the tomato sauce in the centre of the dough. Spread the sauce over the pizza in concentric circles with the back of the ladle, leaving a 2.5 cm (1 in) border clear around the edges for the crust. You only want a thin layer of sauce.

Place a handful of the grated mozzarella in a mound in the middle of the dough. Spread it out evenly across the pizza, leaving the edges clear for the crust. Scatter the diced bacon on top of the cheese, aiming to get a good balance of ingredients across the pizza.

Check there is no liquid on the peel or board or your pizza won't slide off. Shake the board gently to see if the pizza will move. If not, lift up the pizza with a dough cutter or spatula and sprinkle a little flour on the board until it does move easily.

Slide the pizza off the peel or board onto the pizza stone or upside-down baking tray in the hot oven. Cook for about 5 minutes then take it out of the oven, crack the egg directly onto the pizza and slide it back into the oven. If you're worried the egg won't hold its shape, crack it into a small cup, slide the oven rack out a little (keeping it level) and pour the egg into the middle of the pizza, making sure the egg doesn't slide off.

Return to the oven for 2–3 minutes more, until the bottom and crust are golden, the cheese is melted and the egg white is cooked. Take it out of the oven and scatter over the rocket/arugula. Return to the oven for 30–60 seconds, until the greens just start to wilt. Alternatively, skip this step and keep the leaves fresh, letting them wilt only slightly in the residual heat of the pizza. Remove from the oven again and transfer to a wire cooling rack. Allow to stand for 1 minute before cutting into slices.

BACON WITH MOZZARELLA AND BASIL PESTO

It's easy to cure your own bacon. There are two ways of doing it: a dry cure or a wet cure. For a dry cure, you rub salt into pork loin or belly and leave it in the fridge for one or two days, depending on how thick the meat is. For a wet cure, you make a saltwater brine and submerge the pork in it to allow the salt to penetrate the meat by osmosis. I teach a home butchery and charcuterie- and sausage-making course at the cookery school a few times a year and this is one of the things I cover.

2 balls of pizza dough
   (pages 26–35)
pinch of fine sea salt
1 tbsp olive oil
160 ml (⅔ cup) tomato
   sauce (page 44)
250 g (2 cups) grated
   mozzarella
2–3 slices of bacon, cut
   into small dice
2–4 tbsp basil pesto
   (page 52)

*Makes 2 x 25 cm
(10 in) pizzas*

Preheat the oven to 250°C/480°F/gas mark 9 or as high as it will go. Place a pizza stone or an upside-down baking tray in the oven to heat up too. Get all your ingredients and equipment ready, including taking the dough out of the fridge 1 hour before you're ready to cook.

Stretch the pizza dough by hand or roll it out as per the instructions on pages 24–25. Sprinkle a pinch of salt evenly over the dough, then brush a little olive oil onto the rim with a pastry brush to help it turn golden.

Using a ladle or big spoon, pour the tomato sauce in the centre of the dough. Spread the sauce over the pizza in concentric circles with the back of the ladle or spoon, leaving a 2.5 cm (1 in) border clear around the edges for the crust. You only want a thin layer of sauce.

Place a big handful of the grated mozzarella in a mound in the middle of the dough. Use your palm to spread

it out evenly across the pizza, leaving the edges clear for the crust. Scatter the diced bacon on top of the cheese, aiming to get a good balance of ingredients across the pizza.

Check that there is no liquid on the peel or board or your pizza won't slide off it. Shake the board gently to see if the pizza will move. If it doesn't, lift up the pizza with a dough cutter or spatula and sprinkle a little flour on the board until it does move easily.

Slide the pizza off the peel or board onto the pizza stone or upside-down baking tray in the hot oven. Cook for 7–10 minutes, but start checking it after 5 minutes – you want the bottom and the crust to be cooked through and golden and the cheese should be melted.

Take the pizza out of the oven and transfer to a wire cooling rack, then drizzle with the basil pesto. Allow to stand for 1 minute before cutting into slices.

PANCETTA WITH TUSCAN KALE, PARMESAN AND CHILLI OIL

One of the best things about working from the Ballymaloe Cookery School is being able to source fresh produce from our own 100-acre organic farm. It's an incredible luxury to be able to choose ingredients from whatever is ripe and ready to be harvested. Tuscan kale is one of the vegetables that thrives almost all year round in the glasshouses. Also called cavolo nero, do snap some up when you see it. Regular curly kale works on this pizza too, but needs a bit longer in the oven to wilt down.

2 balls of pizza dough
    (pages 26–35)
a few stalks of Tuscan kale
    or curly kale
2 tbsp olive oil
160 ml (²/₃ cup) tomato
    sauce (page 44)
250 g (2 cups) grated
    mozzarella
100 g (3½ oz) pancetta,
    either thinly sliced or
    cut into lardons
2–4 tbsp finely grated
    Parmesan
2–4 tbsp chilli oil
    (page 60)
fine sea salt and freshly
    ground black pepper

Makes 2 x 25 cm
(10 in) pizzas

Preheat the oven to 250°C/480°F/gas mark 9 or as high as it will go. Place a pizza stone or an upside-down baking tray in the oven to heat up too. Get all your ingredients and equipment ready, including taking the dough out of the fridge 1 hour before you're ready to cook.

Cut the kale away from the tough ribs, then chop the tender leaves into bite-sized pieces or slice them into even-sized shreds. Place the kale in a bowl, drizzle with half of the oil and season with salt and pepper. Toss to combine using your hands, until the kale is coated with the oil. This adds extra flavour and also helps protect the kale from the heat of the oven so that it doesn't burn.

Stretch the pizza dough by hand or roll it out as per the instructions on pages 24–25. Sprinkle a pinch of salt evenly over the dough, then brush a little olive oil onto the rim with a pastry brush to help it turn golden.

Using a ladle or big spoon, pour the tomato sauce in the centre of the dough. Spread it over the pizza in concentric circles with the back of the ladle or spoon, leaving a 2.5 cm (1 in) border clear around the edges for the crust. You only want a thin layer of sauce.

Place a handful of the grated mozzarella in a mound in the middle of the dough. Use your palm to spread it out evenly across the pizza, leaving the edges clear for the crust. Scatter the pancetta on top of the cheese, aiming to get a good balance of ingredients across the pizza.

Check that there is no liquid on the peel or board or your pizza won't slide off. Shake the board gently to see if the pizza will move. If it doesn't, lift up the pizza with a dough cutter or spatula and sprinkle a little flour on the board until it does move easily.

Slide the pizza off the peel or board onto the pizza stone or upside-down baking tray in the hot oven. After 4–5 minutes, take it out and scatter the kale evenly across the top. Return the pizza to the oven for about 3–5 minutes more, until the kale has just started to wilt (curly kale needs to cook a little longer than Tuscan kale). You want the bottom and the crust to be cooked through and golden and the cheese should be melted.

Remove from the oven again, transfer to a wire cooling rack, then sprinkle over the grated Parmesan and drizzle with chilli oil. Allow to stand for 1 minute before cutting into slices.

CHORIZO WITH BLUE CHEESE AND ROCKET

There are two ways to make this pizza. If you add the blue cheese for the entire cooking time, it will melt seamlessly into the other toppings. If you would prefer a pizza with a bit more texture, take it out of the oven when there are only a few minutes left to go and add the blue cheese then.

2 balls of pizza dough
(pages 26–35)
2 handfuls of rocket/
arugula
2 tbsp olive oil
pinch of fine sea salt
160 ml (²/₃ cup) tomato
sauce (page 44)
250 g (2 cups) grated
mozzarella
16 slices of dry-cured
chorizo
100 g (³/₄ cup) crumbled
blue cheese

Makes 2 x 25 cm
(10 in) pizzas

Preheat the oven to 250°C/480°F/gas mark 9 or as high as it will go. Place a pizza stone or an upside-down baking tray in the oven to heat up too. Get all your ingredients and equipment ready, including taking the dough out of the fridge 1 hour before you're ready to cook.

Place the rocket/arugula in a bowl. Drizzle with half of the oil and season with a pinch of salt (you don't need any pepper, since the rocket/arugula is so peppery on its own). Toss to combine and coat all the leaves. This adds flavour and helps protect the greens from burning.

Stretch the pizza dough by hand or roll it out as per the instructions on pages 24–25. Sprinkle a pinch of salt evenly over the dough, then brush a little olive oil onto the rim with a pastry brush to help it turn golden.

Using a ladle or big spoon, pour the tomato sauce in the centre of the dough. Spread it over the pizza in concentric circles with the back of the ladle or spoon, leaving a 2.5 cm (1 in) border clear around the edges for the crust. You only want a thin layer of sauce.

Place a big handful of the grated mozzarella in a mound in the middle of the dough. Use your palm to spread it out evenly across the pizza, leaving

the edges clear for the crust. Scatter the chorizo and crumbled blue cheese on top of the mozzarella (or if you would prefer a bit more texture, add the blue cheese later – see the introduction), aiming to get a good balance of ingredients across the pizza.

Check that there is no liquid on the peel or board or your pizza won't slide off. Shake the board gently to see if the pizza will move. If it doesn't, lift up the pizza with a dough cutter or spatula and sprinkle a little flour on the board until it does move easily.

Slide the pizza off the peel or board onto the pizza stone or upside-down baking tray in the hot oven. Cook for 7–10 minutes, but start checking it after 5 minutes – you want the bottom and the crust to be cooked through and golden and the cheese should be melted.

Take the pizza out of the oven and scatter the rocket/arugula evenly across the top. Return the pizza to the oven for only 30 seconds to 1 minute more, until the rocket/arugula has just started to wilt. Alternatively, skip this step to keep the rocket/arugula fresh and let it wilt only slightly in the residual heat of the pizza after it comes out of the oven. Remove from the oven again and transfer to a wire cooling rack. Slice after 1 minute standing.

PARMA HAM WITH ASPARAGUS, BÉCHAMEL, SPRING ONIONS AND PECORINO

Make this pizza in the spring, when asparagus is in season. You can leave the asparagus whole or cut it into 4 cm (1½ in) pieces. Smaller pieces are easier to eat, especially if the spears are thick rather than thin, tender ones, but if you want more of a wow factor, whole spears do look better. Béchamel sauce is a good base for this pizza, but you could use 160 ml (⅔ cup) of the tomato sauce on page 44 instead.

2 balls of pizza dough (pages 26–35)
8–10 spring onions/scallions, roots and green ends removed
2 tbsp olive oil
8–10 asparagus spears, woody ends removed
8–10 tbsp béchamel sauce (page 46)
250 g (2 cups) grated mozzarella
5–6 slices of Parma ham, torn
30 g (⅓ cup) Pecorino shavings
2–4 tbsp hollandaise sauce (page 48) (optional)
fine sea salt and freshly ground black pepper

Makes 2 x 25 cm (10 in) pizzas

Remove the pizza dough from the fridge 1 hour before you're ready to cook. Preheat the oven to 200°C/400°F/gas mark 6.

Place the spring onions/scallions on a baking tray, drizzle with half of the oil and season with salt and pepper. Roast in the oven for 10–12 minutes, until they are starting to get lightly charred.

Raise the oven temperature to 250°C/480°F/gas mark 9 or as high as it will go. Place a pizza stone or an upside-down baking tray in the oven to heat up and get all your ingredients and equipment ready.

Bring a pot of salted water to the boil, then blanch the asparagus spears for 1 minute. Drain immediately and refresh under cold running water.

Stretch the pizza dough by hand or roll it out as per the instructions on pages 24–25. Sprinkle a pinch of salt evenly over the dough, then brush a little olive oil onto the rim with a pastry brush to help it turn golden. Don't brush on too much or the béchamel will slide off when you try to spread it over the dough later.

Using a ladle or big spoon, pour the béchamel in the centre of the dough and spread it over the pizza with the back of the ladle or spoon, leaving 2.5 cm (1 in) clear around the edges. You only want a thin layer of sauce.

Place a big handful of the mozzarella in a mound in the middle of the dough. Spread it out evenly across the pizza, leaving the edges clear for the crust. Scatter the asparagus on top, aiming to get a good balance across the pizza and leaving room to add the spring onions/scallions later on.

Check that there is no liquid on the peel or board or your pizza won't slide off it. Shake the board gently and if the pizza doesn't move, lift it up sprinkle a little flour on the board until it does move easily.

After 6–8 minutes, when the pizza is nearly done, take it out of the oven and scatter over the spring onions/scallions. Return to the oven for 1–2 minutes more, until the bottom and crust are cooked through and golden, the cheese has melted and the spring onions/scallions have heated through again.

Take the pizza out of the oven, then drape the torn slices of Parma ham on top and scatter over the Pecorino shavings. To be really decadent, drizzle hollandaise sauce on top. Slice after 1 minute standing.

SALAMI WITH RED ONION, ROCKET AND RED MUSTARD GREENS MAYONNAISE

Cured meats like salami and pepperoni work best on a pizza when they're thinly sliced. Back in 2009 I worked at the River Café in London for a while and I noticed that Rose Gray, one of the co-founders, was very specific about how thinly she wanted her Parma ham to be cut because she believed it made a big difference to the flavour.

2 balls of pizza dough
  (pages 26–35)
3 tbsp olive oil
1 red onion, thinly sliced
  into rings
2 handfuls of rocket/
  arugula
pinch of fine sea salt
160 ml (⅔ cup) tomato
  sauce (page 44)
250 g (2 cups) grated
  mozzarella
16 slices of salami
2–4 tbsp red mustard
  greens mayonnaise
  (page 51)

*Makes 2 x 25 cm
(10 in) pizzas*

Preheat the oven to 250°C/480°F/gas mark 9 or as high as it will go. Place a pizza stone or an upside-down baking tray in the oven to heat up too. Get all your ingredients and equipment ready, including taking the dough out of the fridge 1 hour before you're ready to cook.

Heat some of the oil in a frying pan set over a medium heat. Add the red onion and cook for about 10 minutes, until the rings have softened but not browned.

Place the rocket/arugula in a bowl. Drizzle with some of the oil and season with a pinch of salt (you don't need any pepper, since the rocket/arugula is so peppery on its own). Toss to combine and coat all the leaves. This adds flavour and helps protect the greens from burning.

Stretch the pizza dough by hand or roll it out as per the instructions on pages 24–25. Sprinkle a pinch of salt evenly over the dough, then brush a little olive oil on the rim to help it turn golden.

Using a ladle or big spoon, pour the tomato sauce in the centre of the dough. Spread it over the pizza in concentric circles with the back of the ladle or spoon, leaving a 2.5 cm (1 in) border clear around the edges for the crust. You only want a thin layer of sauce.

Place a big handful of the mozzarella in a mound in the middle of the dough and spread it out evenly across the pizza, leaving the edges clear for the crust. Scatter the cooked onion rings and salami on top of the cheese, aiming to get a good balance across the pizza.

Check that there is no liquid on the peel or board or your pizza won't slide off. Shake the board gently to see if the pizza will move. If it doesn't, lift it and sprinkle a little flour on the board until it does .

Slide the pizza off the peel or board onto the pizza stone or upside-down baking tray in the hot oven. Cook for 7–10 minutes, but start checking it after 5 minutes – you want the bottom and the crust to be cooked through and golden and the cheese should be melted.

Take the pizza out of the oven and scatter the rocket/arugula across the top. Return the pizza to the oven for only 30 seconds to 1 minute more, until the rocket/arugula has just started to wilt. Alternatively, skip this step to keep the rocket/arugula fresh and let it wilt only slightly in the residual heat of the pizza after it comes out of the oven. Remove from the oven again then drizzle with the red mustard greens mayonnaise. Allow to stand for 1 minute before slicing.

HAM WITH GOUDA AND MAPLE SYRUP

I got the idea for this pizza from an American student who was doing our business course. She was a barista from New York and told us about a pizzeria near her that had this on their menu, so I gave it a try. I've put it on the menu as a special several times now and it's always a hit. I know it sounds like a crazy combination at first, but if you think about it, it's actually pretty similar to bacon with French toast.

2 balls of pizza dough
    (pages 26–35)
pinch of fine sea salt
1 tbsp olive oil
160 ml (²/₃ cup) tomato
    sauce (page 44)
150 g (1¼ cups) grated
    mozzarella
100 g (1 cup) grated
    Dutch Gouda
2–3 large, thin slices of
    cooked ham, chopped
    into bite-sized pieces,
    or 2 slices of bacon,
    cut into small dice
2 tbsp maple syrup

Makes 2 x 25 cm
(10 in) pizzas

Preheat the oven to 250°C/480°F/gas mark 9 or as high as it will go. Place a pizza stone or an upside-down baking tray in the oven to heat up too. Get all your ingredients and equipment ready, including taking the dough out of the fridge 1 hour before you're ready to cook.

Stretch the pizza dough by hand or roll it out as per the instructions on pages 24–25. Sprinkle a pinch of salt evenly over the dough, then brush a little olive oil onto the rim with a pastry brush to help it turn golden.

Using a ladle or big spoon, pour the tomato sauce in the centre of the dough. Spread the sauce over the pizza in concentric circles with the back of the ladle or spoon, leaving a 2.5 cm (1 in) border clear around the edges for the crust. You only want a thin layer of sauce on each pizza.

Place a big handful each of the grated mozzarella and the Gouda in a mound in the middle of the dough. Use your palm to spread it out evenly across the pizza, leaving the edges clear for the crust. Scatter the ham on top of the cheese, aiming to get a good balance of ingredients across the pizza.

Check that there is no liquid on the peel or board or your pizza won't slide off it. Shake the board gently to see if the pizza will move. If it doesn't, lift up the pizza with a dough cutter or spatula and sprinkle a little flour on the board until it does move easily.

Slide the pizza off the peel or board onto the pizza stone or upside-down baking tray in the hot oven. Cook for 7–10 minutes, but start checking it after 5 minutes – you want the bottom and the crust to be cooked through and golden and the cheese should be melted.

Take the pizza out of the oven, transfer to a wire cooling rack and drizzle with the maple syrup. Allow to stand for 1 minute before cutting into slices.

ROAST MEAT PIZZAS

The idea behind all the roast meat pizzas is that you'll use the leftovers from a roast you've made a day or two before rather than roasting an entire chicken or leg of lamb just for the sake of using a little of it on a pizza. Having said that, I've included instructions for how to roast all the meats from scratch in case you need them. When using any kind of leftovers on a pizza, but especially meat, make sure that they are still good to eat and not past their best – a good rule of thumb is that leftover meat stored in the fridge is good for up to three days.

ROAST LEG OF LAMB WITH WILD GARLIC, AIOLI AND SALSA VERDE

The best way to make this pizza is to bake it with the wild garlic, then top it with the thinly sliced roast lamb and the sauces afterwards, so the meat stays succulent.

1 x 2–3 kg (4½–6½ lb) leg of lamb, aitch bone removed (ask your butcher to do this for you)

6 tbsp olive oil

4–5 garlic cloves, sliced

2–3 sprigs of fresh rosemary, broken into tufts

1 bunch of wild garlic/ ramps (see below right) or rocket/arugula

2 balls of pizza dough (pages 26–35)

160 ml (²/₃ cup) tomato sauce (page 44)

250 g (2 cups) grated mozzarella

2–4 tbsp aioli (page 51)

2–4 tbsp salsa verde (page 53)

fine sea salt and freshly ground black pepper

Makes 2 x 25 cm (10 in) pizzas

Take the lamb out of the fridge 1 hour before cooking it and preheat the oven to 230°C/450°F/gas mark 8.

Put the lamb in a roasting tray and drizzle it with 4 tablespoons of the olive oil. Rub the oil all over the meat, either with your hands or using a pastry brush. Season generously with salt and pepper, then cut 2.5 cm (1 in) deep holes all over the lamb and stuff a slice of garlic and a few rosemary leaves into each hole.

Put the lamb into the oven for 15 minutes, then reduce the temperature to 180°C/350°F/ gas mark 4. Cook for another 45 minutes for rare lamb, 60 minutes for medium and 75 minutes for well done. Let the lamb rest for at least 10–15 minutes when it comes out of the oven before carving into thin slices.

To make the pizza, increase the oven temperature to 250°C/480°F/gas mark 9. Place a pizza stone or an upside-down baking tray in the oven to heat up. Get all your ingredients and equipment ready, including taking the dough out of the fridge 1 hour before you're ready to cook.

If the wild garlic leaves are small and tender, toss them in 1 tablespoon of olive oil and a pinch of salt and put them directly onto the pizza. If the leaves are a bit bigger, you may have to cook them beforehand. If that's the case, heat a frying pan over a high heat. Once the pan is really hot, add 1 tablespoon of olive oil and the wild garlic and sprinkle with salt. Cook for a few minutes, stirring constantly. Cook in small batches for best results.

Stretch the pizza dough by hand or roll it out as per the instructions on pages 24–25. Sprinkle a pinch of salt evenly over the dough, then brush the remaining olive oil onto the rim with a pastry brush to help it turn golden.

Using a ladle or big spoon, pour the tomato sauce in the centre of the dough. Spread the sauce over the pizza in concentric circles with the back of the ladle or spoon, leaving a 2.5 cm (1 in) border clear around the edges.

Place a big handful of the grated mozzarella in the middle of the dough and spread it out evenly across the pizza, leaving the edges clear for the crust.

Check that there is no liquid on the peel or board or your pizza won't slide off it. Shake the board gently to see if the pizza will move. If it doesn't, lift up the pizza with a dough cutter or spatula and sprinkle a little flour on the board until it moves easily.

Slide the pizza off the peel or board onto the pizza stone or upside-down baking tray in the hot oven. Cook for 7–10 minutes, but start checking it after 5 minutes – you want the bottom and the crust to be cooked through and golden.

Take the pizza out of the oven and scatter the wild garlic evenly across the top.

Return the pizza to the oven for only 30 seconds to 1 minute more, until the wild garlic has just started to wilt (or to reheat it if you cooked it beforehand). Remove from the oven again and transfer to a wire cooling rack. Scatter over some thinly sliced roast lamb and drizzle with the aioli and salsa verde. Allow to stand for 1 minute before cutting into slices.

Where to find wild garlic

Wild garlic comes out of nowhere in the springtime and it grows in abundance in damp woodlands and near streams, so look there and follow your nose! It's only in season for a short window of time, though, so if you want to have it year round, make it into a wild garlic pesto (page 52) that you can freeze.

VARIATION

Lamb with aubergine /eggplant, tzatziki and horseradish mayonnaise

Prepare the aubergines/eggplants as in the recipe for the aubergine pizza with fennel sauce on page 131, then scatter the slices on top of the mozzarella. When the pizza comes out of the oven, drape some thinly sliced roast lamb on top and drizzle with a couple tablespoons of tzatziki (page 55) and 2–4 tablespoons of horseradish mayonnaise (page 51).

Use the leftover lamb to stuff into pittas with a little wild garlic and tzatziki.

ROAST CHICKEN WITH THYME AND AIOLI

What could be better than a roast chicken dinner on a Friday night, then using the leftovers on a pizza on Saturday? But if you don't have any leftover chicken, you can use one of the recipes below. This is one of our most popular specials at the pizzeria, so I tend to put it on the menu a few times a year.

2 balls of pizza dough
  (pages 26–35)
pinch of fine sea salt
1 tbsp olive oil
160 ml (²/₃ cup) tomato
  sauce (page 44)
250 g (2 cups) grated
  mozzarella
200 g (1½ cups) shredded
  leftover roast chicken
1–2 tsp fresh thyme leaves
2–4 tbsp aioli (page 51)

Makes 2 x 25 cm
(10 in) pizzas

Preheat the oven to 250°C/480°F/gas mark 9 or as high as it will go. Place a pizza stone or an upside-down baking tray in the oven to heat up too. Get all your ingredients and equipment ready, including taking the dough out of the fridge 1 hour before you're ready to cook.

Stretch the pizza dough by hand or roll it out as per the instructions on pages 24–25. Sprinkle a pinch of salt evenly over the dough, then brush a little olive oil onto the rim with a pastry brush to help it turn golden.

Using a ladle or big spoon, pour the tomato sauce in the centre of the dough. Spread the sauce over the pizza in concentric circles with the back of the ladle or spoon, leaving a 2.5 cm (1 in) border clear around the edges.

Place a big handful of the grated mozzarella in a mound in the middle of the dough. Spread it out evenly across the pizza, leaving the edges clear for the crust. Scatter the chicken and thyme on top of the cheese, aiming to get a good balance of ingredients across the pizza.

Check there is no liquid on the peel or board or the pizza won't slide off. Shake the board gently to see if the pizza will move. If it doesn't, lift up the pizza with a dough cutter or spatula and sprinkle a little flour on the board until it moves.

Slide the pizza off the peel or board onto the pizza stone or upside-down baking tray in the hot oven. Cook for 7–10 minutes, but start checking it after 5 minutes – you want the bottom and the crust to be cooked through and golden.

Take the pizza out of the oven and transfer to a wire cooling rack, then drizzle with the aioli. Allow to stand for 1 minute before cutting into slices.

Quick and easy cooked chicken

To roast a chicken breast or thigh: Preheat the oven to 190°C/375°F/gas mark 5. Place a single bone-in, skin-on chicken breast or two bone-in, skin-on chicken thighs on a baking tray. Drizzle with a little olive oil and season generously with salt and pepper, then roast in the oven for 30–40 minutes, until the chicken is fully cooked through.

To poach a chicken breast: Place the chicken in a small saucepan and cover with water. Add ½ teaspoon of salt and aromatics like a smashed garlic clove, a few peppercorns, a bay leaf and one or two sprigs of fresh thyme. Bring to a boil, then reduce the heat to a simmer. Skim off any foam that may have risen to the top, then cover and cook for about 10 minutes, until the chicken is completely cooked through.

BRAISED BEEF WITH BBQ SAUCE, PICKLED RED ONIONS, GREENS AND HORSERADISH MAYONNAISE

Any cut that is suited for slow roasting, like brisket, short ribs or shin, will work well here. The crucial thing is to keep the cooking juices to add to the BBQ sauce. There will be plenty of beef left over, so try it with the pickled onions in quesadillas, tacos or fajitas, or combine the beef and mayo with peppery salad leaves for a fab sandwich.

1 kg (2¼ lb) beef brisket, short ribs or shin, cut into fist-sized pieces (ask your butcher to do this for you)

1 litre (4 cups) beef stock or water

160 ml (⅔ cup) BBQ sauce (page 44)

2 handfuls of greens, such as rocket/arugula, baby spinach, kale, mizuna or mustard greens

2 tbsp olive oil

2 balls of pizza dough (pages 26–35)

250 g (2 cups) grated mozzarella

50 g (⅓ cup) pickled red onions (page 56)

2–4 tbsp horseradish mayonnaise (page 51)

fine sea salt and freshly ground black pepper

Makes 2 x 25 cm (10 in) pizzas

Preheat the oven to 150°C/300°F/gas mark 2.

Season the beef all over with a generous amount of salt and pepper. Place in a casserole/Dutch oven or roasting tin and pour over enough stock or water to cover the beef. Cover the casserole/Dutch oven with a lid or cover the tin tightly with foil and roast for 3 hours, until the beef is meltingly tender. Check on it now and then to make sure the beef isn't drying out and top it up with more stock or water if necessary.

Remove the beef from the oven and carefully pour all the cooking liquid into a large jug or jar. Put the jug in the fridge for 1 hour so the fat can harden, which will make it easier to separate. Tear the beef into shreds when it's cool enough to handle and set aside 125 g (1 cup) for the pizzas.

Increase the oven temperature to 250°C/480°F/gas mark 9. Place a pizza stone or an upside-down baking tray in the oven to heat up too. Get all your other ingredients ready.

Once the fat from the juices has set, skim it off using a spoon and discard it. Pour some of the cooking juices over the shredded beef to moisten it and save 100 ml (⅓ cup + 4 tsp) to use in the BBQ sauce recipe instead of the water.

It's not strictly necessary to do this, but the flavour will be so much better if you do.

Place the greens in a bowl. Drizzle with half the olive oil and season with a pinch of salt. Toss to combine using your hands, until all the greens are coated with the oil. This adds extra flavour and helps protect the greens from the heat of the oven so that they don't burn.

Stretch the pizza dough by hand or roll it out as per the instructions on pages 24–25. Sprinkle a pinch of salt evenly over the dough, then brush the remaining olive oil onto the rim with a pastry brush to help it turn golden.

Using a ladle or big spoon, pour the BBQ sauce in the centre of the dough. Spread the sauce over the pizza in concentric circles with the back of the ladle or spoon, leaving a 2.5 cm (1 in) border clear around the edges for the crust. You only want a thin layer of sauce.

Place a big handful of the grated mozzarella in a mound in the middle of the dough. Spread it out evenly across the pizza, leaving the edges clear for the crust. Scatter the beef and pickled red onions on top of the cheese, aiming to get a good balance of ingredients across the pizza.

Check that there is no liquid on the peel or board or your pizza won't slide off it.

Shake the board gently to see if the pizza will move. If it doesn't, lift up the pizza with a dough cutter or spatula and sprinkle a little flour on the board until it does move easily.

Slide the pizza off the peel or board onto the pizza stone or upside-down baking tray in the oven. Cook for 7–10 minutes, but check it after 5 minutes – you want the bottom and the crust to be cooked through and golden.

Take the pizza out of the oven and scatter the greens evenly across the top. Return the pizza to the oven for only 30 seconds to 1 minute more, until the greens have just started to wilt. Remove from the oven again and transfer to a wire cooling rack, then drizzle with the horseradish mayonnaise. Allow to stand for 1 minute before cutting into slices.

VARIATION

Beef with rocket, horseradish mayonnaise and Béarnaise sauce

Putting horseradish mayonnaise and Béarnaise sauce on the same pizza might sound strange, but putting two sauces on pizzas is really good. Make the pizza as outlined above, but use the tomato sauce on page 44 instead of the BBQ sauce and use only roast beef and rocket/arugula as toppings. Drizzle with 2–4 tablespoons of horseradish mayonnaise (page 51) and 2–4 tablespoons of Béarnaise sauce (page 48) when the pizza comes out of the oven.

ROAST DUCK WITH SPRING ONIONS, SHIITAKE MUSHROOMS AND HOISIN SAUCE

This is an absolute killer of a pizza! Before I even made it I just knew that people would devour it and that it would be the kind of pizza that would get people talking about its unusual but moreish combination of Asian flavours.

2 duck legs or 150 g (1 cup) finely chopped leftover roast duck

15 g (1 tbsp) butter

200 g (3 cups) shiitake mushrooms, thinly sliced

2 balls of pizza dough (pages 26–35)

1 tbsp olive oil

160 ml (²/₃ cup) tomato sauce (page 44)

250 g (2 cups) grated mozzarella

2 spring onions/scallions, thinly sliced on the diagonal

2–4 tbsp hoisin sauce (page 46)

fine sea salt and freshly ground black pepper

Makes 2 x 25 cm (10 in) pizzas

Preheat the oven to 200°C/400°F/gas mark 6. Place the duck legs in a roasting tin and season with salt and pepper. Roast in the oven for 45–50 minutes, until the meat is cooked through. The duck will release a lot of fat, but don't throw it away! Store it in the fridge and use it for roasting potatoes. When the legs are cool enough to handle, remove the skin (you could chop it up and scatter it over the finished pizzas for a crispy, salty hit), then tear the meat off the bones and finely chop it.

Increase the oven temperature to 250°C/480°F/gas mark 9 or as high as it will go. Place a pizza stone or an upside-down baking tray in the oven to heat up. Get all your ingredients and equipment ready, including taking the dough out of the fridge 1 hour before you're ready to cook.

Melt the butter in a large frying pan set over a medium–high heat. Add the mushrooms and cook, stirring often, for about 5 minutes, until they have softened. Set aside.

Stretch the pizza dough by hand or roll it out as per the instructions on pages 24–25. Sprinkle a pinch of salt evenly over the dough, then brush a little olive oil onto the rim with a pastry brush.

Using a ladle or big spoon, pour the tomato sauce in the centre of the dough.

Spread the sauce over the pizza in concentric circles with the back of the ladle or spoon, leaving a 2.5 cm (1 in) border clear around the edges for the crust. You only want a thin layer of sauce.

Place a big handful of the grated mozzarella in a mound in the middle of the dough. Use your palm to spread it out evenly across the pizza, leaving the edges clear for the crust. Scatter the duck and mushrooms on top of the cheese, aiming to get a good balance of ingredients across the pizza.

Check that there is no liquid on the peel or board or your pizza won't slide off it. Shake the board gently to see if the pizza will move. If it doesn't, lift up the pizza with a dough cutter or spatula and sprinkle a little flour on the board until it does move easily.

Slide the pizza off the peel or board onto the pizza stone or upside-down baking tray in the hot oven. Cook for 7–10 minutes, but start checking it after 5 minutes – you want the bottom and the crust to be cooked through and golden and the cheese should be melted.

Take the pizza out of the oven and transfer to a wire cooling rack, then scatter over the spring onions/scallions and drizzle with the hoisin sauce. Allow to stand for 1 minute before cutting into slices.

PORK COOKED IN MILK WITH PECORINO, LEMON AND SAGE

Pork cooked in milk is a classic Italian dish. Most recipes use boneless loin of pork but it can be dry, so I prefer to use shoulder. The leftover pork can be used in ragù, in tacos or stirred into our BBQ sauce on page 44 and served as pulled pork in burger buns.

1 x 1.5 kg (3¼ lb) pork shoulder
4 tbsp olive oil
60 g (4 tbsp) butter
3 garlic cloves, sliced
1 small bunch of fresh sage
1.4 litres (6 cups) whole milk
1½ lemons
2 balls of pizza dough (pages 26–35)
160 ml (⅔ cup) tomato sauce (page 44)
250 g (2 cups) grated mozzarella
30 g (⅓ cup) Pecorino shavings
fine sea salt and freshly ground black pepper

Makes 2 x 25 cm (10 in) pizzas

Remove the rind and trim the fat off the pork shoulder (or ask your butcher to do this for you). Heat 1 tablespoon of the olive oil in a large heavy-bottomed frying pan set over a medium–high heat. Generously season the meat all over with salt and pepper, then add to the pan and brown it on all sides. Set aside.

Melt the butter in a flameproof casserole/Dutch oven that the joint of meat can comfortably fit into. Once it has stopped foaming, add the garlic and about 10 fresh sage leaves and cook for 1 minute, until the garlic is fragrant and has started to brown. Add the pork to the casserole/Dutch oven, then pour in enough milk so that at least three-quarters of the pork is covered (you might need a little more milk). Cut or peel wide strips of zest from the whole lemon and nestle the strips of lemon zest into the milk around the pork. Bring to the boil, then reduce the heat to a gentle simmer. Partly cover the casserole/Dutch oven and simmer for 2–3 hours, without stirring, until the meat is soft and completely cooked through and curds have formed on the surface.

Spoon off the curds, remove the pork and let it rest for at least 10 minutes before carving. Strain the cooking juices through a fine-mesh sieve. To make this pizza, you need to set aside 200 g (1⅓ cups) of finely chopped pork.

To cook the pizzas, preheat the oven to 250°C/480°F/gas mark 9. Place a pizza stone or an upside-down baking tray in the oven to heat up too. Get all your ingredients and equipment ready, including taking the dough out of the fridge 1 hour before you're ready to cook.

Pour 2 tablespoons of olive oil into a small pan and set over a medium–high heat. When the oil is hot, add six fresh sage leaves and fry for a few seconds only, until they turn crisp and deep green. Transfer to a plate lined with paper towels and sprinkle with salt. Repeat with another batch of six sage leaves. Finely grate the zest of the remaining lemon half and set aside.

Stretch the pizza dough by hand or roll it out as per the instructions on pages 24–25. Sprinkle a pinch of salt evenly over the dough, then brush the remaining olive oil onto the rim with a pastry brush to help it turn golden.

Using a ladle or big spoon, pour the tomato sauce in the centre of the dough. Spread the sauce over the pizza in concentric circles with the back of the ladle or spoon, leaving a 2.5 cm (1 in) border clear around the edges for the crust. You only want a thin layer of sauce.

Place a big handful of the grated mozzarella in a mound in the middle of the dough. Spread it out evenly across the pizza, leaving the edges clear for the crust. Scatter the finely chopped pork on top of the mozzarella, aiming to get a good balance across the pizza.

Check that there is no liquid on the peel or board or your pizza won't slide off it. Shake the board gently to see if the pizza will move. If it doesn't, lift up the pizza with a dough cutter or spatula and sprinkle a little flour on the board until it does move easily.

Slide the pizza off the peel or board onto the pizza stone or upside-down baking tray in the hot oven. Cook for 7–10 minutes, but start checking it after 5 minutes – you want the bottom and the crust to be cooked through and golden and the cheese should be melted.

Take the pizza out of the oven and transfer to a wire cooling rack. Scatter over the Pecorino shavings, the finely grated lemon zest and the crispy sage leaves. Allow to stand for 1 minute before cutting into slices.

SLOW-ROASTED PORK WITH CRISPY FRIED SAGE AND TOMATO MAYONNAISE

I like to cook a large pork joint overnight on a Friday so when we come in on Saturday morning, the pork has been slow roasting for 16 hours and just falls apart. This version uses a smaller joint and takes around 4 hours, but you'll still have plenty of leftovers to be stirred into our BBQ sauce on page 44 and served as pulled pork.

1 x 4 kg (8¾ lb) pork shoulder (about half a whole shoulder)
12 large fresh sage leaves
3 tbsp olive oil
2 balls of pizza dough (pages 26–35)
160 ml (²/₃ cup) tomato sauce (page 44)
250 g (2 cups) grated mozzarella
2–4 tbsp tomato mayonnaise (page 51)
fine sea salt and freshly ground black pepper

Makes 2 x 25 cm (10 in) pizzas

If you want to get crispy crackling from your pork shoulder, preheat the oven to 230°C/450°F/gas mark 8. If you won't be using the crackling, preheat the oven to 120°C/250°F/gas mark ½ instead.

Cut deep slashes into the skin of the pork shoulder – a clean Stanley knife does a good job of this. Season the pork generously with salt and pepper, rubbing it right into the slashes. For crackling, place the pork in a large roasting tin and roast in the oven for 30 minutes at 230°C/450°F/gas mark 8, then reduce the heat to 120°C/250°F/gas mark ½ and cook for 3½ hours more, until the meat is meltingly tender and shreds easily. If you don't want to use the crackling, you can put the pork directly in the oven at 120°C/250°F/gas mark ½ and roast it at that temperature for 4 hours instead.

When the pork is done, pour all the roasting juices in the tray into a jug or bowl right away and put the bowl in the fridge. As it cools the fat will rise to the top and harden, which you can then easily spoon off. Leave the meat to cool for about 1 hour, until it's cool enough to handle. You should be able to shred the meat with your hands, making sure there are absolutely no bones, skin or big pieces of fat. Remove the fat from

the cooking juices and stir the juices into the shredded pork and season with a little more salt and pepper. You need 150 g (1 cup) of shredded pork for the pizzas.

When you're ready to cook the pizzas, preheat the oven to 250°C/480°F/gas mark 9 or as high as it will go. Place a pizza stone or an upside-down baking tray in the oven to heat up too. Get all your ingredients and equipment ready, including taking the dough out of the fridge 1 hour before you're ready to cook.

While the oven is heating up again, fry the sage leaves. Pour 2 tablespoons of olive oil into a small pan and set over a medium–high heat. When the oil is hot, add half of the sage leaves and fry for a few seconds only, until they turn crisp and deep green. Transfer to a plate lined with a paper towels and sprinkle with sea salt. Repeat with the remaining sage.

Stretch the pizza dough by hand or roll it out as per the instructions on pages 24–25. Sprinkle a pinch of salt evenly over the dough, then brush the remaining olive oil onto the rim with a pastry brush.

Using a ladle or big spoon, pour the tomato sauce in the centre of the dough. Spread the sauce over the pizza in

concentric circles with the back of the ladle or spoon, leaving a 2.5 cm (1 in) border clear around the edges for the crust. You only want a thin layer of sauce.

Place a big handful of the grated mozzarella in a mound in the middle of the dough. Use your palm to spread it out evenly across the pizza, leaving the edges clear for the crust. Scatter the shredded pork on top of the mozzarella, aiming to get a good balance across the pizza.

Check that there is no liquid on the peel or board or your pizza won't slide off it. Shake the board gently to see if the pizza will move. If it doesn't, lift up the pizza with a dough cutter or spatula and sprinkle a little flour on the board until it does move easily.

Slide the pizza off the peel or board onto the pizza stone or upside-down baking tray in the hot oven. Cook for 7–10 minutes, but start checking it after 5 minutes – you want the bottom and the crust to be cooked through and golden and the cheese should be melted.

Take the pizza out of the oven and transfer to a wire cooling rack. Scatter over the whole crispy sage leaves or crumble them into smaller pieces over the pizza, then drizzle with the tomato mayonnaise. Allow to stand for 1 minute before cutting into slices.

SEAFOOD PIZZAS

Ballymaloe Cookery School is only 5 kilometres from
the fishing village of Ballycotton, so in addition to
our own produce from our organic farm, we also have
access to local seafood fresh off the boat. We really
are spoiled here. In order to make these pizzas turn
out well wherever you are, be sure to use the freshest,
best-quality seafood you possibly can.

ANCHOVIES WITH ROAST RED PEPPERS, RED ONIONS AND KALAMATA OLIVES

It's fine to use a roast pepper from a jar, but if you don't have any on hand or if you'd rather roast one yourself, follow the instructions for the pizza with roast red peppers and cherry tomatoes on page 142.

5 tsp olive oil
1 small red onion, halved and thinly sliced
2 balls of pizza dough (pages 26–35)
pinch of fine sea salt
160 ml (²/₃ cup) tomato sauce (page 44)
250 g (2 cups) grated mozzarella
1 roast red bell pepper (from a jar is fine), cut into bite-sized pieces
10–12 Kalamata olives, pitted and halved
6–8 anchovies in oil, drained

Makes 2 x 25 cm (10 in) pizzas

Preheat the oven to 250°C/480°F/gas mark 9 or as high as it will go. Place a pizza stone or an upside-down baking tray in the oven to heat up too. Get all your ingredients and equipment ready, including taking the dough out of the fridge 1 hour before you're ready to cook.

Heat 2 teaspoons of the olive oil in a frying pan set over a medium heat. Add the red onion and cook for about 10 minutes, until it has softened but not browned.

Stretch the pizza dough by hand or roll it out as per the instructions on pages 24–25. Sprinkle a pinch of salt evenly over the dough, then brush a little of the remaining olive oil onto the rim with a pastry brush to help it turn golden.

Using a ladle or big spoon, pour the tomato sauce in the centre of the dough. Spread the sauce over the pizza in concentric circles with the back of the ladle or spoon, leaving a 2.5 cm (1 in) border clear around the edges for the crust. You only want a thin layer of sauce.

Place a big handful of the grated mozzarella in a mound in the middle of the dough. Use your palm to spread it out evenly across the pizza, leaving the edges clear for the crust. Scatter the cooked red onions, roast peppers, olives and whole anchovies on top of the cheese, aiming to get a good balance of ingredients across the pizza.

Check that there is no liquid on the peel or board or your pizza won't slide off it. Shake the board gently to see if the pizza will move. If it doesn't, lift up the pizza with a dough cutter or spatula and sprinkle a little flour on the board until it does move easily.

Slide the pizza off the peel or board onto the pizza stone or upside-down baking tray in the hot oven. Cook for 7–10 minutes, but start checking it after 5 minutes – you want the bottom and the crust to be cooked through and golden and the cheese should be melted.

Take the pizza out of the oven and transfer to a wire cooling rack. Allow to stand for 1 minute before cutting into slices.

PRAWNS WITH WATERCRESS AND DILL MAYONNAISE

This combination of prawns, watercress and dill mayonnaise also makes a nice starter served with brown soda bread spread thickly with good Irish butter.

2 handfuls of watercress, leaves only

2 tbsp olive oil

15 g (1 tbsp) butter

200 g (7 oz) prawns/shrimp (about 10 per pizza), peeled (ask your fishmonger to do this for you)

2 balls of pizza dough (pages 26–35)

160 ml (⅔ cup) tomato sauce (page 44)

250 g (2 cups) grated mozzarella

2–4 tbsp dill mayonnaise (page 51)

fine sea salt and freshly ground black pepper

Makes 2 x 25 cm (10 in) pizzas

Preheat the oven to 250°C/480°F/gas mark 9 or as high as it will go. Place a pizza stone or an upside-down baking tray in the oven to heat up too. Get all your ingredients and equipment ready, including taking the dough out of the fridge 1 hour before you're ready to cook.

Place the watercress in a bowl. Drizzle with half of the olive oil and season lightly with salt and pepper. Toss to combine using your hands, until all the watercress leaves are coated with the oil. This adds extra flavour and also helps protect the watercress from the heat of the oven so that it doesn't burn.

Stretch the pizza dough by hand or roll it out as per the instructions on pages 24–25. Sprinkle a pinch of salt evenly over the dough, then brush a little olive oil onto the rim with a pastry brush to help it turn golden.

Using a ladle or big spoon, pour the tomato sauce in the centre of the dough. Spread the sauce over the pizza in concentric circles with the back of the ladle or spoon, leaving a 2.5 cm (1 in) border clear around the edges for the crust. You only want a thin layer of sauce.

Place a handful of the grated mozzarella in a mound in the middle of the dough. Spread it out evenly across the pizza, leaving the edges clear for the crust.

Check that there is no liquid on the peel or board or your pizza won't slide off it. Shake the board gently to see if the pizza will move. If it doesn't, lift up the pizza with a dough cutter or spatula and sprinkle a little flour on the board until it does move easily.

Slide the pizza off the peel or board onto the pizza stone or upside-down baking tray in the hot oven. Cook for 7–10 minutes, but start checking it after 5 minutes – you want the bottom and the crust to be cooked through and golden and the cheese should be melted.

While the first pizza is cooking, melt the butter over a medium heat. When it's foaming, tip in the prawns/shrimp and cook for 2–3 minutes, until fully cooked through – they should be firm and white. Remove from the heat and season with a pinch of salt and pepper.

Take the pizza out of the oven and scatter the watercress and prawns/shrimp evenly across the top. Return the pizza to the oven for only 30 seconds to 1 minute more, until the watercress has just started to wilt. Remove from the oven again and transfer to a wire cooling rack, then drizzle with the dill mayonnaise. Allow to stand for 1 minute before cutting into slices.

SMOKED SALMON WITH FRIED CAPERS AND CRÈME FRAÎCHE

This is the kind of pizza where the quality of the ingredients is everything. Use the best smoked salmon you can get, ideally organic and wild rather than farmed. Here at the Ballymaloe Cookery School we use Shanagarry Smoked Salmon, which has been produced just down the road since the 1980s by Bill Casey.

2 tbsp drained capers

3 tbsp olive oil

100 g (3½ oz) good-quality smoked salmon, torn into bite-sized pieces

2 balls of pizza dough (pages 26–35)

pinch of fine sea salt

160 ml (⅔ cup) tomato sauce (page 44)

250 g (2 cups) grated mozzarella

3–4 tbsp crème fraîche

Makes 2 x 25 cm (10 in) pizzas

Preheat the oven to 250°C/480°F/gas mark 9 or as high as it will go. Place a pizza stone or an upside-down baking tray in the oven to heat up too. Get all your ingredients and equipment ready, including taking the dough out of the fridge 1 hour before you're ready to cook.

While the oven is heating up, heat 2 tablespoons of olive oil in a low-sided pan. Pat the capers dry with kitchen paper/paper towels so that the hot oil doesn't splash when you put the capers in. Test the oil by adding one caper – if it sizzles, it's ready. Add all the capers to the hot oil and fry for 1 minute, taking care not to let them burn. Scoop out with a slotted spoon or a small fine-mesh sieve and transfer to a plate lined with paper towels to absorb the excess oil. Set aside – they will crisp up as they dry out.

Stretch the pizza dough by hand or roll it out as per the instructions on pages 24–25. Sprinkle a pinch of salt evenly over the dough, then brush a little olive oil onto the rim with a pastry brush to help it turn golden.

Using a ladle or big spoon, pour the tomato sauce in the centre of the dough. Spread the sauce over the pizza in concentric circles with the back of the ladle or spoon, leaving a 2.5 cm (1 in) border clear around the edges for the crust. You only want a thin layer of sauce.

Place a big handful of the grated mozzarella in a mound in the middle of the dough. Use your palm to spread it out evenly across the pizza, leaving the edges clear for the crust. Scatter the smoked salmon on top of the cheese, aiming to get a good balance across the pizza.

Check that there is no liquid on the peel or board or your pizza won't slide off it. Shake the board gently to see if the pizza will move. If it doesn't, lift up the pizza with a dough cutter or spatula and sprinkle a little flour on the board until it does move easily.

Slide the pizza off the peel or board onto the pizza stone or upside-down baking tray in the hot oven. Cook for 7–10 minutes, but start checking it after 5 minutes – you want the bottom and the crust to be cooked through and golden and the cheese should be melted.

Take the pizza out of the oven and scatter over the fried capers, then drizzle with the crème fraîche (put the crème fraîche in a squeezy bottle if you have one). Allow to stand for 1 minute before cutting into slices.

STEAMED MUSSELS WITH TOMATO SALSA, CORIANDER AND LEMON

Mussels are in season from autumn to spring. Near us here at Shanagarry, they grow wild at Ballyandreen, east of Cork Harbour. Mussels and salsa might sound like an odd combination for a pizza, but it really works. If you're not convinced or mussels are out of season, shredded leftover roast chicken would work too.

1 kg (2¼ lb) mussels
240 ml (1 cup) water
2 balls of pizza dough
   (pages 26–35)
pinch of fine sea salt
1 tbsp olive oil
160 ml (⅔ cup) tomato
   sauce (page 44)
250 g (2 cups) grated
   mozzarella
250 g (1¾ cups) tomato
   salsa (page 59)
½ bunch of fresh
   coriander/cilantro,
   leaves only
zest of ½ lemon

Makes 2 x 25 cm
(10 in) pizzas

Preheat the oven to 250°C/480°F/gas mark 9 or as high as it will go. Place a pizza stone or an upside-down baking tray in the oven to heat up too. Get all your ingredients and equipment ready, including taking the dough out of the fridge 1 hour before you're ready to cook.

Clean the mussels by pulling off any barnacles or beards, then rinsing them in several changes of cold water. Make sure all the mussels are shut. Tap any that are even slightly open on the work surface. If they close, they're safe to eat. If not, they're dead, so discard them.

Pour the water into a large pot, bring to the boil, then tip in the mussels. Cover with a tight-fitting lid and reduce the heat to medium. Steam the mussels for 3–5 minutes, stirring them once or twice, until all the mussels have opened. Discard any that remain closed. Drain the mussels. Once they're cool enough to handle, pick out all the meat.

Stretch the pizza dough by hand or roll it out as per the instructions on pages 24–25. Sprinkle a pinch of salt evenly over the dough, then brush a little olive oil onto the rim to help it turn golden.

Using a ladle or big spoon, pour the tomato sauce in the centre of the dough.

Spread the sauce over the pizza in concentric circles with the back of the ladle or spoon, leaving a 2.5 cm (1 in) border clear around the edges for the crust. You only want a thin layer of sauce.

Place a handful of the grated mozzarella in the middle of the dough. Spread it evenly across the pizza, leaving the edges clear for the crust. Using a slotted spoon to drain excess liquid, add the salsa, making sure it's evenly distributed.

Check that there is no liquid on the peel or board or your pizza won't slide off it. Shake the board gently to see if the pizza will move. If it doesn't, lift it up with a dough cutter or spatula and sprinkle a little flour on the board until it does move easily.

Slide the pizza off the peel or board onto the pizza stone or upside-down baking tray in the hot oven. Cook for 7–10 minutes, but start checking it after 5 minutes – the bottom and the crust should be cooked through and golden and the cheese should be melted.

Take the pizza out of the oven and add the mussels. Return to the oven for 1 minute to heat the mussels. Remove, then scatter over the coriander/cilantro leaves and some lemon zest.

VEGETABLE PIZZAS

You can put any vegetable you want on a pizza, and we do, even unusual things like celeriac or Romanesco broccoli. And if your kids are fussy when it comes to eating veg, maybe they'll eat them on a pizza. It's worth a try!

Vegetables that are in season taste better, so be inspired by what's available at your local market or growing in your own garden. In-season local veg are also more nutritious when at their peak than vegetables that are flown in from halfway around the world. There are few things more rewarding than growing your own veg, even if it's just one or two tomato plants in a pot or some fresh herbs on your windowsill.

MARGHERITA

My wife Emily and I once took the train from Rome to Naples just so we could visit the best pizzeria in the world, L'Antica Pizzeria da Michele. When we arrived there were already two dozen people waiting in line to get into the restaurant and it took us about an hour to be seated. They only serve two types of pizza, a Margherita and a marinara, so we got them both. After we'd eaten, we passed by another famous pizzeria, Pizzeria Trianon, and ordered a pizza from them to take away. We'd been warned about the pickpockets in Naples, but I guarded that pizza more closely than my camera or wallet.

2 balls of pizza dough
   (pages 26–35)
pinch of fine sea salt
1 tbsp shop-bought garlic-
   infused olive oil
160 ml (⅔ cup) tomato
   sauce (page 44)
1 x 125 g (4½ oz) ball
   of fresh mozzarella,
   cut into sugar-cube-
   sized pieces
8–10 fresh basil leaves

*Makes 2 x 25 cm
(10 in) pizzas*

Preheat the oven to 250°C/480°F/gas mark 9 or as high as it will go. Place a pizza stone or an upside-down baking tray in the oven to heat up too. Get all your ingredients and equipment ready, including taking the dough out of the fridge 1 hour before you're ready to cook.

Stretch the pizza dough by hand or roll it out as per the instructions on pages 24–25. Sprinkle a pinch of salt evenly over the dough. Brush a little garlic-infused oil onto the dough with a pastry brush for added flavour, making sure you brush the crust with the oil too.

Using a ladle or big spoon, pour the tomato sauce in the centre of the dough. Spread the sauce over the pizza in concentric circles with the back of the ladle or spoon, leaving a 2.5 cm (1 in) border clear around the edges for the crust. You only want a thin layer of sauce.

Scatter the fresh mozzarella evenly over the pizza, but don't put it too close to the crust or it might melt right off the edge of the pizza.

Check that there is no liquid on the peel or board or your pizza won't slide off it. Shake the board gently to see if the pizza will move. If it doesn't, lift up the pizza with a dough cutter or spatula and sprinkle a little flour on the board until it does move easily.

Slide the pizza off the peel or board onto the pizza stone or upside-down baking tray in the hot oven. Cook for 7–10 minutes, but start checking it after 5 minutes – you want the bottom and the crust to be cooked through and golden and the cheese should be melted.

Take the pizza out of the oven and transfer to a wire cooling rack, then scatter over 4-5 fresh basil leaves. Allow to stand for 1 minute before cutting into slices.

VARIATION

Burrata, cherry tomatoes and truffle oil

Neapolitan pizza-makers might be outraged at the idea of even suggesting a variation on the Margherita, but if you want to take this basic pizza in a more decadent direction, try topping the tomato sauce with some ultra-creamy Burrata cheese and halved cherry tomatoes, then drizzle with truffle oil when the pizza comes out of the oven. Simple but luxurious.

BEETROOT WITH GOATS' CHEESE, MARJORAM AND GREMOLATA

The earthiness of the beetroot is counterbalanced by the creamy goats' cheese and loads of fresh herbs. If you grow your own beetroot/beets or can buy a good selection, try using a mix of colours or varieties to add a real wow factor to this pizza.

2 small or 1 medium beetroot/beets

2–3 sprigs of fresh marjoram, chopped

2 tbsp olive oil

balsamic or apple cider vinegar (optional)

2 balls of pizza dough (pages 26–35)

160 ml (⅔ cup) tomato sauce (page 44)

250 g (2 cups) grated mozzarella

80 g (⅓ cup) Ardsallagh or St Tola goats' cheese (or any other soft goats' cheese)

2–4 tbsp gremolata (page 54)

fine sea salt and freshly ground black pepper

Makes 2 x 25 cm (10 in) pizzas

Preheat the oven to 250°C/480°F/gas mark 9 or as high as it will go. Place a pizza stone or an upside-down baking tray in the oven to heat up too. Get all your ingredients and equipment ready, including taking the dough out of the fridge 1 hour before you're ready to cook.

While the oven is heating up, scrub the unpeeled beetroot really well and boil for 15–20 minutes, depending on size, until just tender when pierced with the tip of a knife. Drain and cool under cold running water. When cool enough to handle, peel the beetroot, but be warned that this will make your hands turn purple!

Slice the beetroot thinly on a mandoline or using a sharp knife and a steady hand. Place the beetroot slices in a bowl with the marjoram, 1 tablespoon of the oil and some salt and pepper. You could add a few drops of balsamic or apple cider vinegar too if you want to add a little tartness.

Stretch the pizza dough by hand or roll it out as per the instructions on pages 24–25. Sprinkle a pinch of salt evenly over the dough, then brush a little olive oil onto the rim with a pastry brush.

Using a ladle or big spoon, pour the tomato sauce in the centre of the dough. Spread the sauce over the pizza in concentric circles with the back of the

ladle or spoon, leaving a 2.5 cm (1 in) border clear around the edges for the crust. You only want a thin layer of sauce.

Place a big handful of the grated mozzarella in a mound in the middle of the dough. Spread it out evenly across the pizza, leaving the edges clear for the crust. Scatter the beetroot slices on top of the cheese, then dot small knobs (about ½ teaspoon each) of the goats' cheese on top, aiming to get a good balance of ingredients across the pizza.

Check there is no liquid on the peel or board or your pizza won't slide off it. Shake the board gently to see if the pizza moves. If it doesn't, lift up the pizza with a dough cutter or spatula and sprinkle a little flour on the board until it moves.

Slide the pizza off the peel or board onto the pizza stone or upside-down baking tray in the hot oven. Cook for 7–10 minutes, but start checking it after 5 minutes – you want the bottom and the crust to be cooked through and golden.

Take the pizza out of the oven and transfer to a wire cooling rack, then sprinkle generously with the gremolata. Allow to stand for 1 minute before cutting into slices.

AUBERGINE WITH FENNEL SAUCE, BLUE CHEESE AND GREMOLATA

Fennel sauce adds a luxurious richness to a pizza. Try it with the toppings suggested in this pizza, or maybe a combination of wild mushrooms, Gruyère and rocket/arugula or even the potato pizza on page 156. But if you prefer, you can always use the tomato sauce on page 44 instead.

1 medium or large
   aubergine/eggplant
3 tbsp olive oil
2 balls of pizza dough
   (pages 26–35)
120 ml (½ cup) fennel
   sauce (page 47)
250 g (2 cups) grated
   mozzarella
100 g (¾ cup) crumbled
   blue cheese
2–4 tbsp gremolata
   (page 54)
fine sea salt and freshly
   ground black pepper

*Makes 2 x 25 cm
(10 in) pizzas*

Preheat the oven to 200°C/400°F/gas mark 6. Line a baking tray with non-stick baking paper.

Cut the aubergine/eggplant into slices 1 cm (½ in) thick. Place all the slices on the lined tray, brush generously with 2 tablespoons of the olive oil and season with salt and pepper. Bake in the oven for about 10 minutes, until they have started to soften. If you don't cook the aubergine/eggplant before adding it to the pizza, it will still be undercooked when it comes out of the oven.

When the aubergines/eggplants come out of the oven, increase the temperature to 250°C/480°F/gas mark 9 or as high as it will go. Place a pizza stone or an upside-down baking tray in the oven to heat up too. Get the rest of your ingredients and equipment ready.

Stretch the pizza dough by hand or roll it out as per the instructions on pages 24–25. Sprinkle a pinch of salt evenly over the dough, then brush a little olive oil onto the rim with a pastry brush to help it turn golden.

Using a ladle or big spoon, pour the fennel sauce in the centre of the dough. Spread the sauce over the pizza in concentric circles with the back of the ladle or spoon, leaving a 2.5 cm (1 in) border clear around the edges for the crust. You only want a thin layer of sauce.

Place a big handful of the grated mozzarella in a mound in the middle of the dough. Use your palm to spread it out evenly across the pizza, leaving the edges clear for the crust. Scatter the aubergine/eggplant slices and blue cheese on top of the mozzarella, aiming to get a good balance of ingredients across the pizza.

Check that there is no liquid on the peel or board or your pizza won't slide off it. Shake the board gently to see if the pizza will move. If it doesn't, lift up the pizza with a dough cutter or spatula and sprinkle a little flour on the board until it does move easily.

Slide the pizza off the peel or board onto the pizza stone or upside-down baking tray in the hot oven. Cook for 7–10 minutes, but start checking it after 5 minutes – you want the bottom and the crust to be cooked through and golden and the cheese should be melted.

Take the pizza out of the oven and transfer to a wire cooling rack, then sprinkle generously with the gremolata. Allow to stand for 1 minute before cutting into slices.

BROAD BEANS WITH BÉCHAMEL, SUN-DRIED TOMATOES AND PARMESAN

Broad/fava beans need a good bit of prep work because you have to peel them twice: once to get them out of their fuzzy pods and then a second time to peel away the thin skin on the bean itself after you've blanched them. Use broad/fava beans when they're young, as later on in the year they can start to take on a floury, mealy texture.

20 fresh broad/fava bean pods
1 tbsp olive oil
2 balls of pizza dough (pages 26–35)
pinch of fine sea salt
8–10 tbsp béchamel sauce (page 46)
250 g (2 cups) grated mozzarella
10 sun-dried tomato halves in oil, drained and chopped
2–4 tbsp finely grated Parmesan

Makes 2 x 25 cm (10 in) pizzas

Preheat the oven to 250°C/480°F/gas mark 9 or as high as it will go. Place a pizza stone or an upside-down baking tray in the oven to heat up too. Get all your ingredients and equipment ready, including taking the dough out of the fridge 1 hour before you're ready to cook.

Bring a pan of water to the boil. Add the beans, cover the pan and cook for 3–5 minutes. Drain and refresh under cold running water, then pop each pod open along its seam and push the beans out. But you're not done yet – next you need to peel off the thin skin on each bean. Place the podded and peeled beans in a bowl and drizzle with half of the oil. This will help to prevent the beans from drying out in the heat of the oven during cooking.

Stretch the pizza dough by hand or roll it out as per the instructions on pages 24–25. Sprinkle a pinch of salt evenly over the dough. Brush a very thin rim of crust with olive oil to help it turn golden. You don't want to brush on too much because the béchamel will slide off it when you try to spread it over the dough later on.

Using a ladle or big spoon, pour 4–5 tablespoons of béchamel in the centre of the dough. Spread the sauce over the pizza in concentric circles with the back

of the ladle or spoon, leaving a 2.5 cm (1 in) border clear around the edges for the crust.

Place a big handful of the grated mozzarella in a mound in the middle of the dough. Use your palm to spread it out evenly across the pizza, leaving the edges clear for the crust. Scatter the podded beans and sun-dried tomatoes evenly over the top of the mozzarella, aiming to get a good balance of ingredients across the pizza.

Check that there is no liquid on the peel or board or your pizza won't slide off it. Shake the board gently to see if the pizza will move. If it doesn't, lift up the pizza with a dough cutter or spatula and sprinkle a little flour on the board until it does move easily.

Slide the pizza off the peel or board onto the pizza stone or upside-down baking tray in the hot oven. Cook for 7–10 minutes, but start checking it after 5 minutes – you want the bottom and the crust to be cooked through and golden and the cheese should be melted.

Take the pizza out of the oven and transfer to a wire cooling rack, then sprinkle over the Parmesan. Allow to stand for 1 minute before slicing.

FENNEL WITH CHILLI, ROCKET AND PECORINO

Pecorino Romano is an aged, salty, hard ewe's milk cheese that is similar to Parmigiano-Reggiano (a cow's milk cheese), but don't be tempted to swap one for the other in equal amounts. Pecorino is a stronger, sharper, saltier cheese than Parmesan. A good guideline is that when using Parmesan instead of Pecorino you will need one and a half times as much.

2 handfuls of rocket/
   arugula
olive oil, to drizzle
½ fennel bulb
½–1 fresh red chilli
2 balls of pizza dough
   (pages 26–35)
160 ml (⅔ cup) tomato
   sauce (page 44)
250 g (2 cups) grated
   mozzarella
30 g (⅓ cup) Pecorino
   shavings or 45 g (scant
   ½ cup) Parmesan
   shavings
fine sea salt and freshly
   ground black pepper

*Makes 2 x 25 cm
(10 in) pizzas*

Preheat the oven to 250°C/480°F/gas mark 9 or as high as it will go. Place a pizza stone or an upside-down baking tray in the oven to heat up too. Get all your ingredients and equipment ready, including taking the dough out of the fridge 1 hour before you're ready to cook.

Place the rocket/arugula in a bowl. Drizzle with olive oil and season with a pinch of salt. Toss to combine using your hands, until all the rocket/arugula leaves are coated with the oil. Cut the green tops off the fennel bulb and discard. Slice the halved fennel bulb as thinly as possible with a mandoline or sharp knife. Place in a bowl, drizzle with olive oil and season with salt and pepper.

Cut the top off the chilli. Turn it upside down and roll it between the palms of your hands – the seeds should all tumble out. Slice it into thin rings or finely dice it. Taste a little bit to see just how hot the chilli is and add it according to your personal taste.

Stretch the pizza dough by hand or roll it out as per the instructions on pages 24–25. Sprinkle a pinch of salt evenly over the dough, then brush a little olive oil onto the rim with a pastry brush to help it turn golden.

Using a ladle or big spoon, pour the tomato sauce in the centre of the dough. Spread the sauce over the pizza in concentric circles with the back of the ladle or spoon, leaving a 2.5 cm (1 in) border clear around the edges for the crust. You only want a thin layer of sauce.

Place a big handful of the grated mozzarella in a mound in the centre of the dough. Use your palm to spread it out evenly across the pizza, leaving the edges clear for the crust. Scatter the sliced fennel and chilli on top.

Check that there is no liquid on the peel or board or your pizza won't slide off it. Shake the board gently to see if the pizza will move. If it doesn't, lift up the pizza with a dough cutter or spatula and sprinkle a little flour on the board until it does move easily.

Slide the pizza off the peel or board onto the pizza stone or upside-down baking tray in the hot oven. Cook the pizza for 7–10 minutes, but start checking it after 5 minutes – you want the bottom and the crust to be cooked through and golden and the cheese should be melted.

Take the pizza out of the oven and scatter the rocket/arugula evenly across the top. Return the pizza to the oven for only 30 seconds to 1 minute, until the rocket/arugula has just started to wilt. Remove from the oven and transfer to a wire cooling rack and scatter over the Pecorino. Allow to stand for 1 minute before slicing.

FLAT MUSHROOMS WITH GARLIC, SPRING ONIONS AND CRÈME FRAÎCHE

The Ballymaloe Cookery School offers seasonal foraging courses with Darina Allen, the school's co-founder, but not everyone is so forthcoming about where to find wild foods. Mushroom foragers are famously secretive about their patches, so if you're not sure where to look, Portobello or large closed cap mushrooms work just as well here.

8–10 spring onions/
   scallions
2 tbsp olive oil
15 g (1 tbsp) butter
4 Portobello mushrooms
   or 8 large closed cap
   mushrooms
2 garlic cloves, finely
   chopped
2 balls of pizza dough
   (pages 26–35)
160 ml (⅔ cup) tomato
   sauce (page 44)
250 g (2 cups) grated
   mozzarella
2–4 tbsp crème fraîche
fine sea salt and freshly
   ground black pepper

*Makes 2 x 25 cm
(10 in) pizzas*

Preheat the oven to 200°C/400°F/gas mark 6. Trim the spring onions/scallions and place on a baking tray. Drizzle with half of the oil and season. Roast for 10–12 minutes, until they are starting to get lightly charred.

Raise the oven temperature to 250°C/480°F/gas mark 9. Place a pizza stone or an upside-down baking tray in the oven to heat up. Get all your ingredients and equipment ready, including taking the dough out of the fridge 1 hour before you're ready to cook.

Wipe the mushrooms clean and remove the stems if necessary, then slice the caps. Melt the butter in a pan set over a medium–high heat, add the mushrooms and season. Cook for 10 minutes, until they have released their juices. Add the garlic and cook for 1 minute more.

Stretch the pizza dough by hand or roll it out as per the instructions on pages 24–25. Sprinkle a pinch of salt over the dough, then brush a little olive oil onto the rim with a pastry brush.

Using a ladle or big spoon, pour the tomato sauce in the centre of the dough. Spread the sauce over the pizza in concentric circles with the back of the ladle or spoon, leaving a 2.5 cm (1 in) border clear around the edges for the crust. You only want a thin layer of sauce.

Place a big handful of the grated mozzarella in a mound in the middle of the dough. Spread it out evenly across the pizza, leaving the edges clear for the crust. Scatter the cooked mushrooms on top of the mozzarella, aiming to get a good balance across the pizza.

Check there is no liquid on the peel or board or your pizza won't slide off it. Shake the board gently to see if the pizza moves. If it doesn't, lift up the pizza with a dough cutter or spatula and sprinkle a little flour on the board until it moves.

Slide the pizza off the peel or board onto the pizza stone or upside-down baking tray in the hot oven. Cook for 6–9 minutes. When the pizza is nearly done, take it out of the oven and scatter over the spring onions/scallions. Return to the oven for 1–2 minutes, until the bottom and crust are cooked through and golden, the cheese has melted and the spring onions/scallions have heated through.

Remove from the oven and transfer to a wire cooling rack, then drizzle with crème fraîche. Allow to stand for 1 minute before slicing.

KALE WITH PARMESAN, EGG AND LEMON

In the winter, when most of the glasshouses at the cookery school are empty, we still have plenty of kale going strong. You can use any kind of kale on this pizza, such as Tuscan kale, curly kale or purple kale. Or if you're growing your own, you could use a mixture of your favourite different types of kale.

a few stalks of kale
2 tbsp olive oil
2 balls of pizza dough
   (pages 26–35)
160 ml (²⁄₃ cup) tomato
   sauce (page 44)
250 g (2 cups) grated
   mozzarella
2 eggs
2–4 tbsp finely grated
   Parmesan
zest of ½ lemon
fine sea salt and freshly
   ground black pepper

*Makes 2 x 25 cm
(10 in) pizzas*

Preheat the oven to 250°C/480°F/gas mark 9. Place a pizza stone or an upside-down baking tray in the oven to heat. Get the ingredients and equipment ready, including taking the dough out of the fridge 1 hour before you're ready to cook.

Cut the kale away from the tough ribs, then chop the leaves into bite-sized pieces. Place the kale in a bowl, drizzle with half of the oil and season with salt and pepper. Toss to combine using your hands and give it a quick massage, until the kale is coated with the oil. This adds flavour and also protects the kale from the heat of the oven so it doesn't burn.

Stretch the pizza dough by hand or roll it out as per the instructions on pages 24–25. Sprinkle a pinch of salt evenly over the dough, then brush a little olive oil onto the rim with a pastry brush.

Using a ladle or big spoon, pour the tomato sauce in the centre of the dough. Spread the sauce over the pizza in concentric circles with the back of the ladle or spoon, leaving a 2.5 cm (1 in) border clear around the edges.

Place a big handful of the grated mozzarella in a mound in the middle of the dough. Spread it out evenly across the pizza, leaving the edges clear.

Check there is no liquid on the peel or board or your pizza won't slide off it.

Shake the board gently to see if the pizza moves. If it doesn't, lift up the pizza with a dough cutter or spatula and sprinkle a little flour on the board until it moves.

Slide the pizza off the peel or board onto the pizza stone or upside-down baking tray in the hot oven. Cook for about 5 minutes.

When the pizza has a few minutes left to go, take it out of the oven and scatter the kale evenly across the top, but leave some empty space in the middle. Crack the egg directly onto the pizza and slide it back into the oven. Or if you're worried about the egg not holding its shape, you can put the pizza back into the oven after adding the kale, then crack the egg into a small cup, slide the oven rack out a little and pour the egg into the middle of the pizza, making sure you keep the rack level. Slide the rack back in and close the door. Cook the pizza for about 3 minutes more, until the kale has just started to wilt (curly kale needs to cook a little longer than Tuscan kale) and the egg white is cooked.

Remove from the oven and transfer to a wire cooling rack, then sprinkle over the grated Parmesan and lemon zest. Allow to stand for 1 minute before slicing.

PEPERONATA AND PARSLEY

Food writers Elizabeth David and Jane Grigson helped bring peperonata to our attention in Ireland and the UK when they wrote about it in their cookbooks. This simple stew of peppers, onion and tomatoes is so versatile, you'll wonder how you ever got by without this recipe in your repertoire, but not surprisingly, my favourite way to use it is on a pizza.

2 balls of pizza dough
(pages 26–35)
pinch of fine sea salt
1 tbsp olive oil
160 ml (⅔ cup) tomato
sauce (page 44)
250 g (2 cups) grated
mozzarella
250 g (1 cup) peperonata
(page 58)
1 tbsp finely chopped
fresh flat-leaf parsley

Makes 2 x 25 cm
(10 in) pizzas

Preheat the oven to 250°C/480°F/gas mark 9 or as high as it will go. Place a pizza stone or an upside-down baking tray in the oven to heat up too. Get all your ingredients and equipment ready, including taking the dough out of the fridge 1 hour before you're ready to cook.

Stretch the pizza dough by hand or roll it out as per the instructions on pages 24–25. Sprinkle a pinch of salt evenly over the dough, then brush the olive oil onto the rim with a pastry brush to help it turn golden.

Using a ladle or big spoon, pour the tomato sauce in the centre of the dough. Spread the sauce over the pizza in concentric circles with the back of the ladle or spoon, leaving a 2.5 cm (1 in) border clear around the edges for the crust. You only want a thin layer of sauce.

Place a big handful of the grated mozzarella in a mound in the middle of the dough. Use your palm to spread it out evenly across the pizza, leaving

the edges clear for the crust. Spoon the peperonata on top of the cheese, aiming to get a good balance of ingredients across the pizza. If the peperonata has a lot of liquid, strain it first so that your pizza doesn't get too soggy.

Check that there is no liquid on the peel or board or your pizza won't slide off it. Shake the board gently to see if the pizza will move. If it doesn't, lift up the pizza with a dough cutter or spatula and sprinkle a little flour on the board until it does move easily.

Slide the pizza off the peel or board onto the pizza stone or upside-down baking tray in the hot oven. Cook for 7–10 minutes, but start checking it after 5 minutes – you want the bottom and the crust to be cooked through and golden and the cheese should be melted.

Take the pizza out of the oven and transfer to a wire cooling rack, then scatter over the parsley. Allow to stand for 1 minute before cutting into slices.

ROAST RED PEPPERS AND CHERRY TOMATOES WITH CROZIER BLUE CHEESE AND ROSEMARY

The handy thing about this pizza is that the peppers roast at the same super-hot temperature that you need to preheat the oven to for the pizzas, but if you're short on time, roasted peppers from a jar would work fine too. The main thing is that the peppers are cooked before you put them on the pizza, otherwise they'll be too crunchy.

Crozier Blue is the sheep's milk version of the famous Cashel Blue cheese made by hand by the Grubb family in County Tipperary on their 200-acre farm and exported all over the world. If you can't source the Crozier Blue, try using the Cashel Blue or any other farmhouse blue cheese instead.

2 red bell peppers
10 cherry tomatoes, halved
1 tbsp olive oil
2 balls of pizza dough (pages 26–35)
160 ml (⅔ cup) tomato sauce (page 44)
250 g (2 cups) grated mozzarella
100 g (¾ cup) crumbled Crozier Blue cheese
2 tsp finely chopped fresh rosemary
fine sea salt and freshly ground black pepper

Makes 2 x 25 cm (10 in) pizzas

Preheat the oven to 250°C/480°F/gas mark 9. Line a baking tray with foil.

Place the whole peppers on the lined tray and roast in the oven for 30–40 minutes, turning them once or twice during that time, until the skins are blackened all over. Remove the peppers from the oven and tightly wrap them in the foil. This will steam the peppers, which makes it easier to peel them. Set aside for about 30 minutes, until the peppers are cool enough to handle, then peel the peppers and remove the stems and seeds. Cut each pepper into thick strips, then cut each strip in half widthways. Set aside.

Once the peppers come out of the oven, place a pizza stone or an upside-down baking tray in the oven to heat up too. Get all your ingredients and equipment ready, including taking the dough out of the fridge 1 hour before you're ready to cook.

Place the halved cherry tomatoes in a bowl. Drizzle with olive oil and season with a generous pinch of salt and pepper.

Stretch the pizza dough by hand or roll it out as per the instructions on pages 24–25. Sprinkle a pinch of salt evenly over the dough, then brush a little olive oil onto the rim with a pastry brush to help it turn golden.

Using a ladle or big spoon, pour the tomato sauce in the centre of the dough. Spread the sauce over the pizza in concentric circles with the back of the ladle or spoon, leaving a 2.5 cm (1 in) border clear around the edges for the crust. You only want a thin layer of sauce.

Place a big handful of the grated mozzarella in a mound in the middle of the dough. Use your palm to spread it out evenly across the pizza, leaving the edges clear for the crust. Scatter the strips of roasted red peppers, cherry tomatoes and crumbled blue cheese on top of the mozzarella, aiming to get a good balance of ingredients across the pizza.

Check that there is no liquid on the peel or board or your pizza won't slide off it. Shake the board gently to see if the pizza will move easily. If it doesn't, lift it with a dough cutter or spatula and sprinkle a little flour on the board until it does move easily.

Slide the pizza off the peel or board onto the pizza stone or upside-down baking tray in the hot oven. Cook for 7–10 minutes, but start checking it after 5 minutes – you want the bottom and the crust to be cooked through and golden and the cheese should be melted.

Take the pizza out of the oven and transfer to a wire cooling rack, then scatter the rosemary across the top. Allow to stand for 1 minute before cutting into slices.

VARIATION

Roast red peppers with Cooleeney Tipperary Brie, red onions and black olives

Omit the cherry tomatoes and rosemary and use 100g (3½ oz) of thinly sliced Cooleeney Brie instead of the blue cheese. Heat a little olive oil in a frying pan set over a medium heat. Add 1 sliced red onion and cook for about 10 minutes, until it has softened but not browned. Add the cooked onions, 10–12 halved pitted black olives and the Brie cheese along with the roast peppers before cooking the pizza as before.

ROAST PUMPKIN WITH FENNEL AND WALNUT PESTO

Even though you only need a small amount of pumpkin for the pizzas, you may as well roast all of it since you're already going to the trouble of preparing it. Cut the pumpkin you'll be using for the pizzas into small cubes, but cut the rest into bigger pieces, place them on a separate baking tray and roast for 25–30 minutes, ready to be added to hearty salads or a risotto, puréed for a soup or made into pumpkin pie.

¼ small pumpkin or butternut squash, peeled and cut into 1 cm (½ in) cubes

olive oil, to drizzle

½ fennel bulb

2 balls of pizza dough (pages 26–35)

160 ml (⅔ cup) tomato sauce (page 44)

250 g (2 cups) grated mozzarella

2–4 tbsp walnut pesto (page 52)

salt and freshly ground black pepper

Makes 2 x 25 cm (10 in) pizzas

Preheat the oven to 200°C/400°F/gas mark 6. Place a pizza stone or an upside-down baking tray in the oven to heat up too. Get all your ingredients and equipment ready, including taking the dough out of the fridge 1 hour before you're ready to cook.

Place the pumpkin on a baking tray, drizzle with olive oil and season with salt and pepper. Roast for about 15 minutes, until tender and starting to brown. When the pumpkin comes out of the oven, raise the temperature to 250°C/480°F/gas mark 9 or as high as it will go.

Cut the green tops off the fennel bulb and discard, but save the fronds as a garnish. Cut the bulb in half, then slice the fennel as thinly as possible. Place in a bowl, drizzle with olive oil and season.

Stretch the pizza dough by hand or roll it out as per the instructions on pages 24–25. Sprinkle a pinch of salt evenly over the dough, then brush a little olive oil onto the rim with a pastry brush to help it turn golden.

Using a ladle or big spoon, pour the tomato sauce in the centre of the dough.

Spread the sauce over the pizza in concentric circles with the back of the ladle or spoon, leaving a 2.5 cm (1 in) border clear around the edges for the crust. You only want a thin layer of sauce.

Place a big handful of the grated mozzarella in a mound in the centre of the dough. Use your palm to spread it out evenly across the pizza, leaving the edges clear for the crust. Scatter the sliced fennel and roast pumpkin on top.

Check that there is no liquid on the peel or board or your pizza won't slide off it. Shake the board gently to see if the pizza will move. If it doesn't, lift up the pizza with a dough cutter or spatula and sprinkle a little flour on the board until it does move easily.

Slide the pizza off the peel or board onto the pizza stone or upside-down baking tray in the hot oven. Cook for 7–10 minutes, but start checking it after 5 minutes – you want the bottom and the crust to be cooked through and golden.

Take the pizza out of the oven and transfer to a wire cooling rack. Drizzle with the walnut pesto and garnish with the fennel fronds. Allow to stand for 1 minute before cutting into slices.

RED ONION JAM WITH BLUE CHEESE, BLACK OLIVES AND GREMOLATA

We have a regular customer at the pizzeria who likes to put all the ingredients from the specials, regardless of what they are, on one pizza. He can't decide, so he has it all – like this unusual combination. He used to insist that I make his pizza rather than any of my staff. One time I was so busy that I couldn't do it, so I told the person who was making his pizza to just put all the toppings we had that day on it and to add extra salt and pepper. Later that night I met our customer in the pub and he was raving about the pizza, saying it was the best one ever, so I had to confess that I hadn't actually made it that day.

2 balls of pizza dough
(pages 26–35)
pinch of fine sea salt
1 tbsp olive oil
160 ml (²/₃ cup) tomato
sauce (page 44)
250 g (2 cups) grated
mozzarella
6 heaped tbsp red onion
jam (page 57)
100 g (³/₄ cup) crumbled
blue cheese
10–12 black olives, pitted
and halved
2–4 tbsp gremolata
(page 54)

Makes 2 x 25 cm
(10 in) pizzas

Preheat the oven to 250°C/480°F/gas mark 9 or as high as it will go. Place a pizza stone or an upside-down baking tray in the oven to heat up too. Get all your ingredients and equipment ready, including taking the dough out of the fridge 1 hour before you're ready to cook.

Stretch the pizza dough by hand or roll it out as per the instructions on pages 24–25. Sprinkle a pinch of salt evenly over the dough, then brush a little olive oil onto the rim with a pastry brush to help it turn golden.

Using a ladle or big spoon, pour the tomato sauce in the centre of the dough. Spread the sauce over the pizza in concentric circles with the back of the ladle or spoon, leaving a 2.5 cm (1 in) border clear around the edges for the crust. You only want a thin layer of sauce.

You have two options now: you can either add a thin layer of the red onion jam directly on top of the dough, to be covered up by the mozzarella, or you can dollop spoonfuls of the jam on top of the cheese. Either way, place a big handful of the grated mozzarella in a mound in the middle of the dough. Use your palm to spread it out evenly across the pizza, leaving the edges clear for the crust. Dollop spoonfuls of the red onion jam on top of the mozzarella if you haven't already spread it directly on the base, then scatter over the blue cheese and the halved olives.

Check that there is no liquid on the peel or board or your pizza won't slide off it. Shake the board gently to see if the pizza will move. If it doesn't, lift up the pizza with a dough cutter or spatula and sprinkle a little flour on the board until it does move easily.

Slide the pizza off the peel or board onto the pizza stone or upside-down baking tray in the hot oven. Cook for 7–10 minutes, but start checking it after 5 minutes – you want the bottom and the crust to be cooked through and golden and the cheese should be melted.

Take the pizza out of the oven and transfer it to a wire cooling rack, then scatter the gremolata evenly over the pizza. Allow it to stand for 1 minute before cutting into slices.

COURGETTE WITH POUNDED PARSLEY AND GARLIC OIL

If you grow your own, like we do here at the cookery school, courgettes/zucchini can be a mixed blessing. On the one hand, they grow like mad. On the other hand, well, they grow like mad! Here's one way to use some up when you've run out of ideas and inspiration for a glut from your garden or they're in season and cheap to buy.

1 large courgette/zucchini
2 balls of pizza dough (pages 26–35)
pinch of fine sea salt
1 tbsp olive oil
160 ml (⅔ cup) tomato sauce (page 44)
250 g (2 cups) grated mozzarella
2–4 tbsp pounded parsley and garlic oil (page 61)

Makes 2 x 25 cm (10 in) pizzas

Preheat the oven to 250°C/480°F/gas mark 9 or as high as it will go. Place a pizza stone or an upside-down baking tray in the oven to heat up too. Get all your ingredients and equipment ready, including taking the dough out of the fridge 1 hour before you're ready to cook.

Using a Y-shaped vegetable peeler, peel the courgette/zucchini into wide ribbons.

Stretch the pizza dough by hand or roll it out as per the instructions on pages 24–25. Sprinkle a pinch of salt evenly over the dough, then brush a little olive oil onto the rim with a pastry brush to help it turn golden.

Using a ladle or big spoon, pour the tomato sauce in the centre of the dough. Spread the sauce over the pizza in concentric circles with the back of the ladle or spoon, leaving a 2.5 cm (1 in) border clear around the edges for the crust. You only want a thin layer of sauce.

Place a big handful of the grated mozzarella in a mound in the middle of the dough. Use your palm to spread it out evenly across the pizza, leaving the edges clear for the crust. Drape the courgette/zucchini ribbons on top of the cheese, aiming to get a good balance of ingredients across the pizza.

Check that there is no liquid on the peel or board or your pizza won't slide off it. Shake the board gently to see if the pizza will move. If it doesn't, lift up the pizza with a dough cutter or spatula and sprinkle a little flour on the board until it does move easily.

Slide the pizza off the peel or board onto the pizza stone or upside-down baking tray in the hot oven. Cook for 7–10 minutes, but start checking it after 5 minutes – you want the bottom and the crust to be cooked through and golden and the cheese should be melted.

Take the pizza out of the oven and transfer to a wire cooling rack, then drizzle with the pounded parsley and garlic oil. Allow to stand for 1 minute before cutting into slices.

GOATS' CHEESE AND RED ONIONS WITH ROCKET AND CHILLI OIL

Ardsallagh goats' cheese is made by the Murphy family in Carrigtwohill in County Cork – Jane Murphy sometimes comes to the cookery school to talk to the students. The St Tola cheese made near the Burren in County Clare is wonderful too. Both have won lots of national and international awards over the years and both are available nationwide. Any soft goats' cheese works well, but these two are my favourites.

2 tbsp olive oil

1 small red onion, halved and thinly sliced

2 handfuls of rocket/ arugula

pinch of fine sea salt

2 pizza dough balls (pages 26–35)

160 ml (⅔ cup) tomato sauce (page 44)

250 g (2 cups) grated mozzarella

80 g (⅓ cup) Ardsallagh or St Tola soft goats' cheese (or any other soft goats' cheese)

2–4 tbsp chilli oil (page 60)

Makes 2 x 25 cm (10 in) pizzas

Preheat the oven to 250°C/480°F/gas mark 9. Place a pizza stone or an upside-down baking tray in the oven to heat up. Get the ingredients and equipment ready, including taking the dough out of the fridge 1 hour before you're ready to cook.

Heat 1 tablespoon of the oil in a frying pan set over a medium heat. Add the red onion and cook for about 10 minutes, until it has softened.

Place the rocket/arugula in a bowl. Drizzle with 1 tablespoon of the oil and season with a pinch of salt, then toss until the leaves are coated. This adds flavour and helps protect them from the heat of the oven so they don't burn.

Stretch the pizza dough by hand or roll it out as per the instructions on pages 24–25. Sprinkle a pinch of salt evenly over the dough, then brush a little olive oil onto the rim with a pastry brush.

Using a ladle or big spoon, pour the tomato sauce in the centre of the dough. Spread the sauce over the pizza in concentric circles with the back of the ladle or spoon, leaving a 2.5 cm (1 in) border clear around the edges.

Place a big handful of the grated mozzarella in a mound in the middle of the dough. Spread it out evenly across the pizza, leaving the edges clear for the crust. Scatter the onions on top, then dot small knobs (about ½ teaspoon each) of the goats' cheese over, aiming to get a balance of ingredients across the pizza.

Check there is no liquid on the peel or board or your pizza won't slide off it. Shake the board gently to see if the pizza moves. If it doesn't, lift up the pizza with a dough cutter or spatula and sprinkle a little flour on the board until it moves.

Slide the pizza off the peel or board onto the pizza stone or upside-down baking tray in the hot oven. Cook for 7–10 minutes, but start checking it after 5 minutes – you want the bottom and the crust to be cooked through and golden.

Take the pizza out of the oven and scatter over the rocket/arugula. Return the pizza to the oven for 30 seconds to 1 minute more, until the rocket/arugula has just started to wilt. You can skip this step if you'd like to keep the leaves fresh and let them wilt in the residual heat of the pizza after it comes out of the oven. Remove from the oven and transfer to a wire cooling rack, then drizzle with the chilli oil. Allow to stand for 1 minute before slicing.

GOATS' CHEESE WITH GUACAMOLE, TOASTED SOURDOUGH BREADCRUMBS AND ROCKET

I first came across breadcrumbs as a pizza topping when I worked in the River Café in London. I know this combination of toppings sounds a little strange, but they served this pizza as a staff meal once and I loved the crunch that the crumbs added to the texture.

Breadcrumbs are sometimes called poor man's Parmesan (or *pangrattato* in Italian, which translates simply as 'grated bread'). Fresh breadcrumbs fried in butter or olive oil until they're golden and crispy, tossed with chopped herbs, salt and pepper and maybe a little lemon zest, dried chilli/hot red pepper flakes, chopped garlic or anchovies make a great topping on pasta, risotto, casseroles, salads, vegetable sides, soups and, yes, pizza.

1–2 slices of day-old
    sourdough bread
3 tbsp olive oil
2 handfuls of rocket/
    arugula
2 balls of pizza dough
    (pages 26–35)
160 ml (2/3 cup) tomato
    sauce (page 44)
250 g (2 cups) grated
    mozzarella
80 g (1/3 cup) Ardsallagh
    or St Tola soft goats'
    cheese (or any other
    soft goats' cheese)
1 batch of guacamole
    (page 59)
fine sea salt and freshly
    ground black pepper

*Makes 2 x 25 cm
(10 in) pizzas*

Preheat the oven to 250°C/480°F/gas mark 9 or as high as it will go. Place a pizza stone or an upside-down baking tray in the oven to heat up too. Get all your ingredients and equipment ready, including taking the dough out of the fridge 1 hour before you're ready to cook.

Cut the bread into small cubes, then place in a food processor and blitz into fine breadcrumbs. Heat 1 tablespoon of the olive oil in a frying pan over a medium heat, then add the breadcrumbs and season with a good pinch of salt and pepper. Fry the breadcrumbs for 8–10 minutes, stirring regularly, until they are golden brown and crisp, taking care not to let them burn. Tip out onto a plate and allow to cool.

Place the rocket/arugula in a bowl. Drizzle with 1 tablespoon of the oil and season with a pinch of salt (you don't need any pepper, since the rocket/arugula is so peppery on its own). Toss to combine using your hands, until all the rocket/arugula leaves are coated with the oil. This adds extra flavour and also helps

protect the rocket/arugula from the heat of the oven so that it doesn't burn.

Stretch the pizza dough by hand or roll it out as per the instructions on pages 24–25. Sprinkle a pinch of salt evenly over the dough, then brush a little olive oil onto the rim with a pastry brush to help it turn golden.

Using a ladle or big spoon, pour the tomato sauce in the centre of the dough. Spread the sauce over the pizza in concentric circles with the back of the ladle or spoon, leaving a 2.5 cm (1 in) border clear around the edges for the crust. You only want a thin layer of sauce.

Place a big handful of the grated mozzarella in a mound in the middle of the dough. Spread it out evenly across the pizza, leaving the edges clear for the crust. Dot small knobs (about 1/2 teaspoon each) of the goats' cheese on top of the mozzarella. Aim to get a balance of ingredients across the pizza.

Check that there is no liquid on the peel or board or your pizza won't slide off it.

Shake the board gently to see if the pizza will move. If it doesn't, lift up the pizza with a dough cutter or spatula and sprinkle a little flour on the board until it does move easily.

Slide the pizza off the peel or board onto the pizza stone or upside-down baking tray in the hot oven. Cook for 7–10 minutes, but start checking it after 5 minutes –

you want the bottom and the crust to be cooked through and golden and the cheese should be melted.

Take the pizza out of the oven and transfer to a wire cooling rack. Dollop the guacamole on top and scatter over the toasted breadcrumbs, then add a handful of the dressed rocket/arugula and let it wilt slightly in the residual heat of the pizza. Allow to stand for 1 minute before slicing.

CELERIAC WITH GUBBEEN CHEESE AND AIOLI

Knobbly, ugly and long overlooked, celeriac is having a bit of a moment. It's usually served raw in a remoulade, where it keeps its crisp, celery-like flavour, but like all root vegetables, it roasts beautifully too. Even though you only need a little bit for the pizza, go ahead and roast the rest to use in soups or wintertime salads or to add to a mix of other roasted root veg, like carrots, parsnips and swedes/rutabagas.

Gubbeen is a semi-soft, rind-washed cheese made from the milk of the Ferguson family's own herd of cows on their farm in Schull, County Cork. With flavour notes of nuts and mushrooms, it's a good match for the roasted celeriac. If you can't get Gubbeen, use blue cheese instead, which is also a good match with celeriac.

¼ small head of celeriac, peeled and cut into small cubes

2 tbsp olive oil

2 balls of pizza dough (pages 26–35)

160 ml (⅔ cup) tomato sauce (page 44)

250 g (2 cups) grated mozzarella

100 g (⅔ cup) small cubes of Gubbeen cheese or crumbled blue cheese

2–4 tbsp aioli (page 51)

fine sea salt and freshly ground black pepper

Makes 2 x 25 cm (10 in) pizzas

Preheat the oven to 200°C/400°F/gas mark 6.

Place the celeriac on a baking tray, drizzle with 1 tablespoon of the oil and season with salt and pepper. Toss well to make sure all the celeriac is coated with the oil and seasoning. Roast in the oven for about 15 minutes, until the celeriac is tender when pierced with the tip of a knife.

When the celeriac comes out of the oven, raise the temperature to 250°C/480°F/gas mark 9 or as high as it will go. Place a pizza stone or an upside-down baking tray in the oven to heat up too. Get the rest of your ingredients and equipment ready.

Stretch the pizza dough by hand or roll it out as per the instructions on pages 24–25. Sprinkle a pinch of salt evenly over the dough, then brush a little olive oil onto the rim with a pastry brush to help it turn golden.

Using a ladle or big spoon, pour the tomato sauce in the centre of the dough. Spread the sauce over the pizza in concentric circles with the back of the ladle or spoon, leaving a 2.5 cm (1 in) border clear around the edges for the crust. You only want a thin layer of sauce.

Place a big handful of the grated mozzarella in a mound in the middle of the dough. Use your palm to spread it out evenly across the pizza, leaving the edges clear for the crust. Scatter the roast celeriac and Gubbeen cheese on top of the mozzarella, aiming to get a good balance of ingredients across the pizza.

Check that there is no liquid on the peel or board or your pizza won't slide off it. Shake the board gently to see if the pizza will move. If it doesn't, lift up the pizza with a dough cutter or spatula and sprinkle a little flour on the board until it does move easily.

Slide the pizza off the peel or board onto the pizza stone or upside-down baking tray in the hot oven. Cook for 7–10 minutes, but start checking it after 5 minutes – you want the bottom and the crust to be cooked through and golden.

Take the pizza out of the oven and transfer to a wire cooling rack, then drizzle with the aioli. Allow to stand for 1 minute before cutting into slices.

POTATO WITH GRUYÈRE, WILD GARLIC AND GREMOLATA

Given how much the Irish love potatoes, I don't know why it's not a more popular pizza topping here. After all, it's a popular pizza in Rome (*pizza con patate*) and there's even a restaurant called Bar in New Haven, Connecticut, whose speciality is a mashed potato pizza. Don't knock it till you've tried it! This pizza also works well with the fennel sauce on page 47 if you want a change from the usual tomato sauce.

3 medium potatoes, unpeeled (about 375 g/13 oz)
olive oil, to drizzle
1 bunch of wild garlic/ ramps or rocket/arugula (see page 103 for where to find wild garlic)
2 balls of pizza dough (pages 26–35)
160 ml (2/3 cup) tomato sauce (page 44)
250 g (2 cups) grated mozzarella
100 g (1 heaped cup) grated Gruyère cheese
2–4 tbsp gremolata (page 54)
fine sea salt and freshly ground black pepper

Makes 2 x 25 cm (10 in) pizzas

Preheat the oven to 200°C/400°F/gas mark 6. Line a baking tray with non-stick baking paper.

Slice the potatoes as thinly as you can – a mandoline or the slicing attachment of a food processor are perfect for this. Place them in a bowl and toss with olive oil and some salt and pepper. Place the potato slices on the lined tray in an even layer and roast for 7 minutes, until the edges are just starting to turn golden. Slide a spatula under the potatoes as soon as they come out of the oven, otherwise they might stick to the paper when you try to remove them later on.

Turn the oven temperature up to 250°C/480°F/gas mark 9 or as high as it will go. Place a pizza stone or an upside-down baking tray in the oven to heat up. Get all your ingredients and equipment ready, including taking the dough out of the fridge 1 hour before you're ready to cook.

If the wild garlic leaves are small and tender, you can just toss them in olive oil and a pinch of salt and put them directly onto the pizza and cook it in the oven. If the leaves are a bit bigger and tougher, you may have to cook them beforehand. If that's the case, heat a frying pan over a high heat. Once the pan is really hot,

add 1 tablespoon of olive oil and a good handful of wild garlic and sprinkle with salt. Cook for a few minutes, stirring constantly. Once the leaves don't puff up anymore, you can take them out of the pan and set aside. Cook in small batches at a time for better results.

Stretch the pizza dough by hand or roll it out as per the instructions on pages 24–25. Sprinkle a pinch of salt evenly over the dough, then brush a little olive oil onto the rim with a pastry brush.

Using a ladle or big spoon, pour the tomato sauce in the centre of the dough. Spread the sauce over the pizza in concentric circles with the back of the ladle or spoon, leaving a 2.5 cm (1 in) border clear around the edges.

Place a big handful of the grated mozzarella in a mound in the middle of the dough, then add the Gruyère. Use your palm to spread the cheeses out evenly across the pizza, leaving the edges clear for the crust. Scatter the potatoes on top of the cheese, aiming to get a balance of ingredients across the pizza.

Check that there is no liquid on the peel or board or your pizza won't slide off it. Shake the board gently to see if the pizza moves easily. If it doesn't, lift up the pizza with a dough cutter or spatula and sprinkle a little flour on the board until it does move easily.

Slide the pizza off the peel or board onto the pizza stone or upside-down baking tray in the hot oven. Cook for 7–10 minutes, but start checking it after 5 minutes – you want the bottom and the crust to be cooked through and golden and the cheese should be melted.

Take the pizza out of the oven and scatter over the wild garlic. Return the pizza to the oven for 30 seconds to 1 minute, until the wild garlic just starts to wilt (or to reheat if you cooked it). Remove from the oven and place on a wire cooling rack, then sprinkle over the gremolata. Stand for 1 minute before cutting into slices.

Potato with blue cheese and rosemary

Add 100 g (¾ cup) of crumbled blue cheese instead of the Gruyère. To make this a more pared-back pizza, you could even skip the mozzarella and use only blue cheese. Sprinkle the pizza with a pinch of finely chopped fresh rosemary when it comes out of the oven.

WILD NETTLES WITH HOMEMADE RICOTTA AND PECORINO

Darina Allen runs foraging courses at the cookery school and we always serve the students a pizza with foraged ingredients that we've collected ahead of time, such as wild garlic, watercress or even a seaweed aioli. This nettle pizza is always a hit.

When they're still young and tender, nettles don't have much of a sting. Even so, you always need to wear thick gloves when you harvest them and handle them with tongs until they have been blanched, which takes away the sting. If nettles are out of season, use a few handfuls of lightly wilted baby spinach instead.

1 large bunch of young wild nettles, leaves picked, or baby spinach
2 balls of pizza dough (pages 26–35)
1 tbsp olive oil
160 ml (2/3 cup) tomato sauce (page 44)
250 g (2 cups) grated mozzarella
60 g (1/4 cup) homemade ricotta (page 49)
30 g (1/3 cup) Pecorino shavings
fine sea salt

Makes 2 x 25 cm (10 in) pizzas

Preheat the oven to 250°C/480°F/gas mark 9 or as high as it will go. Place a pizza stone or an upside-down baking tray in the oven to heat up too. Get all your ingredients and equipment ready, including taking the dough out of the fridge 1 hour before you're ready to cook.

Bring a pan of salted water to the boil. Using tongs, add the nettles to the boiling water and blanch for 10 seconds, then drain and refresh under cold running water. Blanching removes their sting, so don't be afraid to handle them now.

Stretch the pizza dough by hand or roll it out as per the instructions on pages 24–25. Sprinkle a pinch of salt evenly over the dough, then brush a little olive oil onto the rim with a pastry brush.

Using a ladle or big spoon, pour the tomato sauce in the centre of the dough. Spread the sauce over the pizza in concentric circles with the back of the ladle or spoon, leaving a 2.5 cm (1 in) border clear around the edges for the crust. You only want a thin layer of sauce.

Place a big handful of the grated mozzarella in a mound in the middle of the dough. Use your palm to spread it out evenly across the pizza, leaving the edges clear for the crust. Using a teaspoon, dot small spoonfuls of the ricotta on top of the mozzarella, aiming to get a good balance of ingredients across the pizza.

Check that there is no liquid on the peel or board or your pizza won't slide off it. Shake the board gently to see if the pizza will move. If it doesn't, lift up the pizza with a dough cutter or spatula and sprinkle a little flour on the board until it does move easily.

Slide the pizza off the peel or board onto the pizza stone or upside-down baking tray in the hot oven. Cook for 7–10 minutes, but start checking it after 5 minutes – you want the bottom and the crust to be cooked through and golden and the cheese should be melted.

Take the pizza out of the oven and scatter over the blanched nettle leaves. Return to the oven for 30 seconds to 1 minute more, then remove from the oven again and scatter over the Pecorino shavings. Transfer to a wire cooling rack and allow to stand for 1 minute before slicing.

ROMANESCO WITH CHILLI FLAKES, PARMESAN AND SALSA VERDE (THE REGGIE SPECIAL)

Reggie is a larger-than-life guy, a friend of a friend who came to Ballymaloe to do the 12-week cookery course. It turns out his brother has a pizza place in San Francisco and Reggie often talked about wanting to open his own pizzeria too someday, so needless to say, we got along great. One day I went on social media to ask people for suggestions of what to serve as the vegetarian special in Saturday Pizzas that week, and this is the winning combination that Reggie came up with.

1 small head of
   Romanesco or regular
   broccoli, broken into
   small, even-sized florets
olive oil, to drizzle
2 balls of pizza dough
   (pages 26–35)
250 g (2 cups) grated
   mozzarella
50 g (1 cup) finely grated
   Parmesan
½–1 tsp dried chilli/hot
   red pepper flakes
2–4 tbsp salsa verde
   (page 53)
fine sea salt

*Makes 2 x 25 cm
(10 in) pizzas*

Preheat the oven to 250°C/480°F/gas mark 9 or as high as it will go. Place a pizza stone or an upside-down baking tray in the oven to heat up too. Get all your ingredients and equipment ready, including taking the dough out of the fridge 1 hour before you're ready to cook.

Bring a pan of salted water to the boil. Add the Romanesco florets and blanch them for 1–2 minutes. Drain and refresh under cold running water, then place in a bowl. Drizzle with olive oil and season with salt.

Stretch the pizza dough by hand or roll it out as per the instructions on pages 24–25. Sprinkle a pinch of salt evenly over the dough, then brush a little olive oil onto the rim with a pastry brush to help it turn golden.

Place a big handful of the grated mozzarella in a mound in the middle of the dough (there is no sauce on this pizza). Use your palm to spread it out evenly across the pizza, leaving the edges clear for the crust. Sprinkle a thick layer of the grated Parmesan on top of the mozzarella, then scatter over the Romanesco broccoli and dried chilli/hot red pepper flakes, aiming to get a good balance of ingredients across the pizza.

Check that there is no liquid on the peel or board or your pizza won't slide off it. Shake the board gently to see if the pizza will move. If it doesn't, lift up the pizza with a dough cutter or spatula and sprinkle a little flour on the board until it does move easily.

Slide the pizza off the peel or board onto the pizza stone or upside-down baking tray in the hot oven. Cook for 7–10 minutes, but start checking it after 5 minutes – you want the bottom and the crust to be cooked through and golden and the cheese should be melted.

Take the pizza out of the oven and transfer to a wire cooling rack, then drizzle over some salsa verde. Allow to stand for 1 minute before slicing.

PEAS WITH HOMEMADE RICOTTA, MINT AND LEMON

We have a small milking parlour and dairy at the cookery school where we milk our own Jersey cows and make our own cheeses, but anyone can make ricotta (see page 49).

75 g (½ cup) frozen peas
olive oil, to drizzle
pinch of fine sea salt
2 balls of pizza dough
    (pages 26–35)
160 ml (⅔ cup) tomato
    sauce (page 44)
250 g (2 cups) grated
    mozzarella
60 g (¼ cup) homemade
    ricotta (page 49)
1–2 sprigs of fresh mint,
    leaves roughly torn
zest of ½ lemon

*Makes 2 x 25 cm
(10 in) pizzas*

Preheat the oven to 250°C/480°F/gas mark 9 or as high as it will go. Place a pizza stone or an upside-down baking tray in the oven to heat up too. Get all your ingredients and equipment ready, including taking the dough out of the fridge 1 hour before you're ready to cook.

Bring a small pan of salted water to the boil. Add the peas and blanch for 20 seconds, then drain and refresh under cold running water to keep their bright green colour. Transfer to a bowl and toss with a little olive oil and a pinch of salt.

Stretch the pizza dough by hand or roll it out as per the instructions on pages 24–25. Sprinkle a pinch of salt evenly over the dough, then brush a little olive oil onto the rim with a pastry brush to help it turn golden.

Using a ladle or big spoon, pour the tomato sauce in the centre of the dough. Spread the sauce over the pizza in concentric circles with the back of the ladle or spoon, leaving a 2.5 cm (1 in) border clear around the edges for the crust. You only want a thin layer of sauce.

Place a big handful of the grated mozzarella in a mound in the middle of the dough. Use your palm to spread it out evenly across the pizza, leaving the edges clear for the crust. Using a teaspoon, dot small spoonfuls of the ricotta on top of the mozzarella, aiming to get a good balance of ingredients across the pizza.

Check there is no liquid on the peel or board or your pizza won't slide off it. Shake the board to see if the pizza will move. If it doesn't, lift up the pizza with a dough cutter or spatula and sprinkle a little flour on the board until it moves.

Slide the pizza off the peel or board onto the pizza stone or upside-down baking tray in the hot oven. Cook for 6 minutes, then take it out of the oven and scatter the peas on top so that they get embedded in the melted cheese. Put the pizza back in the oven for anywhere from 1 to 4 minutes more, until the bottom and the crust are cooked through and golden.

Take the pizza out of the oven and transfer to a wire cooling rack, then sprinkle over the mint and lemon zest. Allow to stand for 1 minute before slicing.

VARIATION

Peas with goats' cheese, Parmesan and mint

Make as per the recipe above, but use 80 g (⅓ cup) of soft goats' cheese instead of the ricotta. When the pizza comes out of the oven, sprinkle with 2–4 tablespoons of finely grated Parmesan and scatter over some finely chopped fresh mint.

CALZONES + PANZEROTTI

A calzone is basically a covered pizza baked in the shape of a turnover or half moon and it's usually eaten with a knife and fork – think of it as an Italian version of a Cornish pasty. Delicious by themselves, sometimes we ladle a bit of extra tomato sauce and chopped fresh herbs on top of the calzone when it comes out of the oven. They are also really good dipped into a bowl of sauce served alongside.

Panzerotti are smaller than calzones and are usually deep-fried. Originating in 18th-century Naples, panzerotti are sometimes called *pizze fritte* ('fried pizzas'). In the States, you might see something similar called pizza puffs or pizza pockets. Panzerotti are ideal for children's birthday parties, school lunches or picnics. For a grown-up get-together, panzerotti make wonderful little nibbles, especially when you use more refined fillings, like the beef with Béarnaise sauce on page 66.

Like the toppings on a pizza, the possibilities for calzone and panzerotti fillings are endless, but here are a few of our favourites.

CALZONE WITH HOMEMADE SAUSAGE, FRESH MOZZARELLA AND BABY SPINACH

You can use any of the homemade sausage recipes on pages 64–65 in this calzone. For a quicker, easier option if you are pushed for time, buy your favourite good-quality butcher sausages and squeeze the meat out of the casings.

2 balls of pizza dough
    (pages 26–35)
olive oil, for shallow frying
100 g (½ cup) sausage
    meat (see recipe
    introduction)
semolina, for dusting
120 ml (½ cup) tomato
    sauce (page 46)
1 x 125 g (4½ oz) ball of
    fresh mozzarella, cut
    into sugar-cube-sized
    pieces
2 handfuls of baby
    spinach

Makes 2 calzones

Preheat the oven to 250°C/480°F/gas mark 9 or as high as it will go. Place a pizza stone or an upside-down baking tray in the oven to heat up too. Get all your ingredients and equipment ready, including taking the dough out of the fridge 1 hour before you're ready to cook.

While the oven is heating up, warm sufficient oil for shallow frying in a frying pan set over a medium–low heat. Roll the sausage meat into walnut-sized balls and cook until they have just browned all over. Using a slotted spoon, transfer to a plate lined with paper towels to absorb any excess oil.

Stretch the pizza dough by hand or roll it out as per the instructions on pages 24–25. Sprinkle the pizza peel or a thin wooden cutting board with semolina, then put the dough on top.

Spread a thin layer of tomato sauce over the bottom half of the dough to within 2.5 cm (1 in) of the edge. Place the mozzarella cubes over the sauce, then scatter over the parcooked sausage meat and top with a handful of baby spinach.

Brush the edge of the dough with water, fold the top half over the fillings on the bottom and seal the edges by pressing them tightly together with your fingers or crimp them with the tines of a fork – we do this by giving them karate chops all the way around the edge. The main thing is to make sure it's tightly sealed so that the steam can't escape and prevent the calzone from puffing up. Brush the top with cold water.

Make sure there is no liquid on the peel or board or your calzone won't slide off it. Shake the board gently to see if the calzone will move. If it doesn't, lift up the calzone with a dough cutter or spatula and sprinkle a little flour on the board until it does move easily.

Slide the calzone off the peel or board onto the pizza stone or upside-down baking tray in the hot oven. Bake for 8–10 minutes, until the dough is cooked through and golden and it has puffed up. As soon as the calzone comes out of the oven, brush the top with a little olive oil. A steak knife is handy for cutting the calzone in half, but watch out for the steam that will escape when you do.

CALZONE WITH PARMA HAM, BLUE CHEESE AND BABY SPINACH

You can't go wrong with this classic combination of Parma ham, blue cheese and baby spinach. It's definitely on the salty side, so serve with a cold craft beer to cut through the strong flavours. A stout or porter works really well with salty toppings and fillings and is a good match with blue cheese.

2 balls of pizza dough
   (pages 26–35)
semolina, for dusting
120 ml (½ cup) tomato
   sauce (page 44)
125 g (1 cup) grated
   mozzarella
100 g (¾ cup) crumbled
   blue cheese
4–5 slices of Parma ham,
   torn
2 handfuls of baby
   spinach
olive oil, for brushing

Makes 2 calzones

Preheat the oven to 250°C/480°F/gas mark 9 or as high as it will go. Place a pizza stone or an upside-down baking tray in the oven to heat up too. Get all your ingredients and equipment ready, including taking the dough out of the fridge 1 hour before you're ready to cook.

Stretch the pizza dough by hand or roll it out as per the instructions on pages 24–25. Sprinkle the pizza peel or thin wooden cutting board with semolina, then put the dough on top.

Spread a thin layer of tomato sauce over the bottom half of the dough to within 2.5 cm (1 in) of the edges. Scatter the mozzarella over the sauce, then scatter over the blue cheese and Parma ham and top with a handful of the baby spinach.

Brush the edge of the dough with water, fold the top half over the fillings on the bottom and seal the edges by pressing them tightly together with your fingers or crimp them with the tines of a fork –

we do this by giving them karate chops all the way around the edge. The main thing is to make sure it's tightly sealed so that the steam can't escape and prevent the calzone from puffing up. Brush the top with cold water.

Make sure there is no liquid on the peel or board or your calzone won't slide off it. Shake the board gently to see if the calzone will move. If it doesn't, lift up the calzone with a dough cutter or spatula and sprinkle a little flour on the board until it does move easily.

Slide the calzone off the peel or board onto the pizza stone or upside-down baking tray in the hot oven. Bake for 8–10 minutes, until the dough is cooked through and golden and it has puffed up. As soon as the calzone comes out of the oven, brush the top with a little olive oil. A steak knife is handy for cutting the calzone in half, but watch out for the steam that will escape when you do.

CALZONE WITH HAM, MUSHROOMS, GRUYÈRE AND GARDEN GREENS

Sometimes we like to make smaller calzones, which are easier to eat without a knife and fork. My brother and I make ones like this to take to football matches. If you want to try making these smaller calzones, cut the rolled-out dough in half with a pizza cutter to create wedge-shaped calzones instead of half-moons.

2 balls of pizza dough
    (pages 26–35)
250 g (9 oz) mushrooms
15 g (1 tbsp) butter
semolina, for dusting
120 ml (½ cup) tomato
    sauce (page 44),
    plus extra for serving
    (optional)
100 g (1 cup) grated
    Gruyère
100 g (⅔ cup) finely
    chopped cooked ham
2 handfuls of garden
    greens, such as baby
    spinach, baby kale or
    rocket/arugula
2 tsp chopped fresh
    flat-leaf parsley
fine sea salt and freshly
    ground black pepper

Makes 2 calzones

Preheat the oven to 250°C/480°F/gas mark 9 or as high as it will go. Place a pizza stone or an upside-down baking tray in the oven to heat up too. Get all your ingredients and equipment ready, including taking the dough out of the fridge 1 hour before you're ready to cook.

While the oven is heating up, wipe the mushrooms clean and remove the stems, then slice the caps. Melt the butter in a pan set over a medium–high heat. When it stops foaming, add the sliced mushrooms and season with salt and pepper. Cook for about 10 minutes, until they have released their juices and are deeply flavourful.

Stretch the pizza dough by hand or roll it out as per the instructions on pages 24–25. Sprinkle the pizza peel or a thin wooden cutting board with semolina, then put the dough on top.

Spread a thin layer of tomato sauce over the bottom half of the dough to within 2.5 cm (1 in) of the edge. Scatter the grated Gruyère over the sauce, then top with the ham, mushrooms and a handful of greens.

Brush the edge of the dough with water, fold the top half over the fillings on the bottom and seal the edges by pressing them tightly together with your fingers or crimp them with the tines of a fork – we do this by giving them a karate chop all the way around the edge. The main thing is to make sure it's tightly sealed so that the steam can't escape and prevent the calzone from puffing up. Brush the top with cold water.

Make sure there is no liquid on the peel or board or your calzone won't slide off it. Shake the board gently to see if the calzone will move. If it doesn't, lift up the calzone with a dough cutter or spatula and sprinkle a little flour on the board until it does move easily.

Slide the calzone off the peel or board onto the pizza stone or upside-down baking tray in the hot oven. Bake for 8–10 minutes, until the dough is cooked through and golden and it has puffed up. As soon as the calzone comes out of the oven, brush the top with a little olive oil and spoon over a little tomato sauce if you like, then sprinkle over the parsley. Use a steak knife to cutting the calzone in half, but watch out for the escaping steam.

PANZEROTTI

Panzerotti are made with a basic yeast dough in Italy, but at the cookery school we have even made them with our native Irish white soda bread. When it comes to fillings, use your imagination and whatever you have in your fridge – just make sure they are generously seasoned. You can go for a traditional combination like mozzarella, tomatoes and basil, or try something more unusual, like cream cheese, smoked salmon and a pinch of dill. Some Italian chefs are even experimenting with sweet versions now, like chocolate or fresh fruit. They can be baked or deep-fried and are a delicious snack or party food.

sunflower oil, for deep-frying (optional)
1 ball of pizza dough (pages 26–35)
fine sea salt and freshly ground black pepper
olive oil or egg wash (1 egg beaten with 1 tbsp water or milk), for brushing if baking

For the tomato and mozzarella filling:
1 large, ripe tomato, peeled, deseeded and finely chopped
1 x 125 g (4¼ oz) ball of fresh mozzarella, drained and cut into tiny pieces
a few fresh basil leaves, torn

For the salami filling:
6 slices of salami or pepperoni, finely diced
1 large, ripe tomato, peeled, deseeded and finely chopped
1 tbsp finely grated Parmesan
a few fresh basil leaves, torn

For the smoked salmon filling:
1 tbsp cream cheese
100 g (½ cup) finely diced smoked salmon
pinch of dried or finely chopped fresh dill

Makes 6

To bake the panzerotti, preheat the oven to 230°C/450°F/gas mark 8 and line a baking sheet with non-stick baking paper. To deep-fry them, heat 7.5 cm (3 in) worth of sunflower oil in a deep fat fryer or a high-sided, heavy-based saucepan to 190°C (375°F).

Following the instructions on pages 24–25, roll out the pizza dough, but this time roll it out as thinly as possible. Cut into six discs with a 10 cm (4 in) cutter or the rim of a small bowl, then using a well-floured rolling pin, roll out each disc a bit more.

For the tomato and mozzarella filling and the salami filling, mix all the ingredients together in a small bowl and season generously with salt and pepper. Fill the bottom half of each disc of dough with a generous tablespoon of well-seasoned filling.

For the smoked salmon filling, spread ½ teaspoon of cream cheese over the bottom half of each disc, then top with 1 tablespoon of diced salmon and a pinch of dill.

Brush the edge of each disc with cold water, fold over into a half-moon shape and seal securely with your fingers or press with the tines of a fork. If baking, pop onto the lined baking tray, brush the tops with olive oil or egg wash and bake for 12–15 minutes, until the dough is cooked through and golden brown.

Alternatively, slide a few at a time (unglazed) into the hot oil. Cook for about 5 minutes, turning them over halfway through, until golden. Drain on a plate lined with paper towels and serve immediately.

FRUIT + DESSERT PIZZAS

Fruit works really well on a pizza, and I don't mean the common but controversial combination of ham and pineapple. I love to add autumn fruits like apples, pears and figs as toppings, since their natural sweetness contrasts perfectly with salty cheese.

The two dessert pizzas in this section are purely a bit of a fun. Try making them the next time you're throwing a kids' birthday party – or a party for grown-ups, for that matter! Whatever the average age of your guests, I guarantee they'll be a big hit.

FIGS WITH GOATS' CHEESE, ROCKET AND HONEY

Don't miss your chance to make this classy pizza when figs are in season. Because there is no sauce, use the best fruit, cheese and honey you can find. If you'd like a sauce, the tomato (page 44) or fennel (page 47) would both work well.

2 balls of pizza dough
    (pages 26–35)
2 handfuls of rocket/
    arugula
2 tablespoons olive oil
4 fresh figs, each sliced
    into eighths
80 g (⅓ cup) soft
    goats' cheese
    (we use Ardsallagh
    goats' cheese)
runny honey, for drizzling
fine sea salt

*makes 2 x 25 cm
(10 inch) pizzas*

Preheat the oven to 250°C/480°F/gas mark 9 or as high as it will go. Place a pizza stone or an upside-down baking tray in the oven to heat up too. Get all your ingredients and equipment ready, including taking the dough out of the fridge 1 hour before you're ready to cook.

Place the rocket/arugula in a bowl. Drizzle with a little olive oil and season with a pinch of salt (there's no need for pepper). Toss to coat all the leaves with the oil. This adds extra flavour and also helps protect the rocket/arugula from the heat of the oven so that it doesn't burn.

Place the figs in a separate bowl and drizzle with a little olive oil. Toss gently to make sure all the figs are lightly coated with oil, handling carefully so they don't break up.

Stretch the pizza dough by hand or roll it out as per the instructions on pages 24–25. Sprinkle a pinch of salt evenly over the dough, then brush all over with a really nice olive oil to help it turn golden.

Scatter the figs on top of the dough, then dot small knobs (about ½ teaspoon each) of the goats' cheese between the figs, aiming to get a good balance of ingredients across the pizza.

Check that there is no liquid on the peel or board or your pizza won't slide off it. Shake the board gently to see if the pizza will move. If it doesn't, lift up the pizza with a dough cutter or spatula and sprinkle a little flour on the board until it does move easily.

Slide the pizza off the peel or board onto the pizza stone or upside-down baking tray in the hot oven. Cook for 7–10 minutes, but start checking after 5 minutes – you want the dough to be cooked through and golden. The figs should be soft and will have started to release their juices and the goats' cheese may be slightly charred in places.

Take the pizza out of the oven. Drizzle with honey and scatter the rocket/arugula evenly across the top. Return the pizza to the oven for only 30 seconds to 1 minute more, until the rocket/arugula has just started to wilt. Alternatively, skip this step and add the honey and rocket/arugula when the pizza is done – the rocket/arugula will still wilt slightly from the residual heat of the pizza. Remove from the oven again and transfer to a wire cooling rack. Allow to stand for 1 minute before cutting into slices.

CARAMELIZED APPLE WITH BLUE CHEESE AND CANDIED WALNUTS

In the fruit garden at the cookery school we grow many heirloom varieties of apples, including Irish Peach, Beauty of Bath and American Mother. I can think of few better pizzas to make when the apples have just been harvested, than this one. The sweetness of the lightly caramelized apples and candied walnuts contrasts perfectly with the salty blue cheese. It's especially good served with a craft stout or brown ale.

2 balls of pizza dough
  (pages 26–35)
30 g (2 tbsp) butter
60 g (¼ cup) + 1 tbsp
  sugar
100 g (1 cup) walnut
  halves
2 sweet dessert apples,
  peeled, cored and
  thinly sliced
pinch of fine sea salt
1 tbsp olive oil
160 ml (⅔ cup) tomato
  sauce (page 44)
250 g (2 cups) grated
  mozzarella
100 g (¾ cup) crumbled
  blue cheese

Makes 2 x 25 cm (10 in) pizzas

Preheat the oven to 250°C/480°F/gas mark 9 or as high as it will go. Place a pizza stone or an upside-down baking tray in the oven to heat up too. Get all your ingredients and equipment ready, including taking the dough out of the fridge 1 hour before you're ready to cook.

To make the candied walnuts, place a large piece of non-stick baking paper on the work surface. Melt half the butter in a frying pan set over a medium heat. Once the butter has stopped foaming, stir in the 60 g (¼ cup) of sugar, then add the walnuts. Cook for about 5 minutes, stirring regularly and taking care not to let the walnuts burn, until the sugar has dissolved and the walnuts are all coated. Working fast, tip the walnuts out onto the paper and use a spatula to quickly separate the nuts. Leave to cool for about 10 minutes, until hardened, then roughly chop the nuts.

Meanwhile, melt the remaining butter in a frying pan set over a medium heat. Add the apple slices and the tablespoon of sugar and cook for about 10 minutes, until the apples are golden brown and soft but still keeping their shape.

Stretch the pizza dough by hand or roll it out as per the instructions on pages 24–25. Sprinkle a pinch of salt evenly over the dough, then brush a little olive oil onto the rim to help it turn golden.

Using a ladle or big spoon, pour the tomato sauce in the centre of the dough. Spread it over the pizza in concentric circles with the back of the ladle or spoon, leaving 2.5 cm (1 in) clear around the edges for the crust. You only want a thin layer of sauce.

Place a handful of the mozzarella in the middle of the dough and spread it out evenly across the pizza, leaving the edges clear for the crust. Scatter the apples and blue cheese on top, aiming to get a good balance of ingredients across the pizza.

Slide the pizza onto the pizza stone or tray in the hot oven. Cook for 7–10 minutes, but start checking it after 5 minutes – the bottom and crust should be cooked through and golden and the cheese should be melted.

Take the pizza out of the oven, then sprinkle over the candied walnuts. Stand for 1 minute before cutting into slices.

SHAVED APPLE WITH BLACK PUDDING AND WHOLEGRAIN MUSTARD MAYONNAISE

Black pudding is one of our more unorthodox pizza toppings, but this is one of those fusion food combinations – Irish black pudding on an Italian pizza – that really works. In the early 1980s Alice Waters was one of the first people to experiment with unusual, non-traditional pizza toppings after she built her wood-burning oven at Chez Panisse. This anything-goes approach eventually became known as California-style pizza. There's even a restaurant in San Francisco, Zante Pizza and Indian Cuisine, that puts an Indian spin on pizza with offerings like chicken tikka pizza or paneer pizza with masala sauce. As the Zante owner, Dalvinder Multani, says, 'You can put anything you want on a pizza'.

2 balls of pizza dough
  (pages 26–35)
200 g (11 oz) black
  pudding
1 sweet dessert apple,
  cored and shaved
  into slices using a
  mandoline or very
  thinly sliced
1 apple
pinch of fine sea salt
1 tbsp olive oil
160 ml (²/₃ cup) tomato
  sauce (page 44)
250 g (2 cups) grated
  mozzarella
2–4 tbsp wholegrain
  mustard mayonnaise
  (page 51)

Makes 2 x 25 cm
(10 in) pizzas

Preheat the oven to 250°C/480°F/gas mark 9 or as high as it will go. Place a pizza stone or an upside-down baking tray in the oven to heat up too. Get all your ingredients and equipment ready, including taking the dough out of the fridge 1 hour before you're ready to cook.

Remove the black pudding casing and discard it, then either crumble it into walnut-sized pieces or thinly slice. Use the shaved apple slices fresh, or you could caramelize them as on page 179, to bring out the sweetness to set against the earthiness of the black pudding.

Stretch the pizza dough by hand or roll it out as per the instructions on pages 24–25. Sprinkle a pinch of salt evenly over the dough, then brush a little olive oil onto the rim with a pastry brush to help it turn golden.

Using a ladle or big spoon, pour the tomato sauce in the centre of the dough. Spread it over the pizza in concentric circles with the back of the ladle or spoon, leaving 2.5 cm (1 in) clear around the edges for the crust. You only want a thin layer of sauce.

Place a big handful of the grated mozzarella in a mound in the middle of the dough. Use your palm to spread it out evenly across the pizza, leaving the edges clear for the crust. Scatter the black pudding and shaved apples on top of the cheese, aiming to get a good balance of ingredients across the pizza.

Check that there is no liquid on the peel or board or your pizza won't slide off it. Shake the board gently to see if the pizza will move. If it doesn't, lift it up with a dough cutter or spatula and sprinkle a little flour on the board until it does move easily.

Slide the pizza off the peel or board onto the pizza stone or upside-down baking tray in the hot oven. Cook for 7–10 minutes, but start checking it after 5 minutes – you want the bottom and the crust to be cooked through and golden and the cheese should be melted.

Take the pizza out of the oven and transfer to a wire cooling rack, then drizzle with the wholegrain mustard mayonnaise. Allow to stand for 1 minute before cutting into slices.

PEARS WITH FETA, WALNUTS AND ROCKET

I like the sharp tang of the feta cheese against the sweetness of the pears instead of the classic combination of blue cheese and pears, but that would work just as well.

2 balls of pizza dough
    (pages 26–35)
2 small ripe pears, cored
    and sliced
2 tablespoons olive oil
2 handfuls of rocket/
    arugula
pinch of fine sea salt
160 ml (⅔ cup) tomato
    sauce (page 44)
250 g (2 cups) grated
    mozzarella
100 g (½ cup) cubed feta
50 g (½ cup) walnut
    halves, roughly chopped

Makes 2 x 25 cm
(10 in) pizzas

Preheat the oven to 250°C/480°F/gas mark 9 or as high as it will go. Place a pizza stone or an upside-down baking tray in the oven to heat up too. Get all your ingredients and equipment ready, including taking the dough out of the fridge 1 hour before you're ready to cook.

Place the pear slices in a bowl and brush with a little olive oil. Place the rocket/arugula in another bowl, drizzle with a little olive oil and season with a pinch of salt (there's no need for pepper). Toss to coat all the leaves with the oil. This adds extra flavour and also helps protect the rocket/arugula from the heat of the oven so that it doesn't burn.

Stretch the pizza dough by hand or roll it out as per the instructions on pages 24–25. Sprinkle a pinch of salt evenly over the dough, then brush a little olive oil onto the rim with a pastry brush to help it turn golden.

Using a ladle or big spoon, pour the tomato sauce in the centre of the dough. Spread it over the pizza in concentric circles with the back of the ladle or spoon, leaving a 2.5 cm (1 in) border clear around the edges for the crust. You only want a thin layer of sauce.

Place a big handful of the grated mozzarella in a mound in the middle of the dough. Use your palm to spread it out evenly across the pizza, leaving the edges clear for the crust. Scatter the pear slices, feta and walnuts on top of the mozzarella, aiming to get a good balance of ingredients across the pizza.

Check that there is no liquid on the peel or board or your pizza won't slide off it. Shake the board gently to see if the pizza will move. If it doesn't, lift it up with a dough cutter or spatula and sprinkle a little flour on the board until it does move easily.

Slide the pizza off the peel or board onto the pizza stone or upside-down baking tray in the hot oven. Cook for 7–10 minutes, but start checking it after 5 minutes – you want the bottom and the crust to be cooked through and golden and the cheese should be melted.

Take the pizza out of the oven and scatter the rocket/arugula evenly across the top. Return the pizza to the oven for only 30 seconds to 1 minute more, until the rocket/arugula has just started to wilt. Alternatively, you can skip this step if you'd like to keep the rocket/arugula fresh and let it wilt only slightly in the residual heat of the pizza after it comes out of the oven. Remove from the oven again and transfer to a wire cooling rack. Allow to stand for 1 minute before cutting into slices.

CHOCOLATE-HAZELNUT SPREAD WITH MARSHMALLOWS AND TOASTED HAZELNUTS

My nephew's friend Rowen has started working with me a few days a week and he helped me develop this recipe. He liked it so much that he told all his friends about the Nutella pizza and it wasn't long before they were all asking when I was going to add it to the pizzeria's menu.

2 balls of chocolate pizza
    dough (page 36)
4 tbsp whole blanched
    hazelnuts
2 tbsp chocolate-hazelnut
    spread, such as Nutella
1 tbsp milk
80 g (2 cups) mini
    marshmallows

Makes 2 x 25 cm
(10 in) pizzas

Get all your ingredients and equipment ready, including taking the dough out of the fridge 1 hour before you're ready to cook. Preheat the oven to 200°C/400°F/gas mark 6.

Place the hazelnuts on a baking sheet and spread them out in an even layer. Roast in the hot oven for 8–10 minutes, until toasted and golden brown. Tip out onto a plate and allow to cool, then roughly chop and set aside.

When the hazelnuts come out of the oven, increase the temperature to 250°C/480°F/gas mark 9 or as high as it will go.

Place the chocolate-hazelnut spread and milk in a small bowl and whisk until smooth, adding a little more milk if necessary to achieve a good drizzling consistency.

Roll out the dough as per the instructions on page 25 (the chocolate dough is too stiff to stretch by hand). Prick the dough all over with the tines of a fork so that it doesn't puff up too much in the oven, since it's being baked on its own without any toppings.

Slide the dough off the peel or board onto the pizza stone or upside-down baking tray in the hot oven. Cook the bases on their own for 4 minutes, then remove from the oven and scatter the mini marshmallows across the bases in an even layer, leaving a 2.5 cm (1 in) border clear around the edges for the crust. Cook for 3 minutes more, until the dough is cooked through and the marshmallows have started to melt and are golden brown on top. Once the marshmallows have been added, don't cook the pizza for more than a few minutes or the marshmallows will disintegrate.

Take the pizza out of the oven and transfer to a wire cooling rack. Drizzle over the Nutella, then scatter over the chopped hazelnuts. Allow to stand for 1 minute before cutting into slices, ideally using a long chef's knife instead of a pizza cutter to make it easier to cut through the gooey marshmallows.

BANOFFEE PIZZA

Banoffee pie is a classic British dessert made with a biscuit/cookie base topped with bananas, whipped cream and toffee – in fact, the name is a combination of the words 'banana' and 'toffee'. I figured if it works as a pie, why not try it as a pizza?

2 balls of chocolate pizza
    dough (page 36)
300 ml (1¼ cups) double/
    heavy cream
4 bananas, sliced
4 tbsp toffee sauce
    (page 61)
1 small bar of milk or
    dark chocolate

Makes 2 x 25 cm
(10 in) pizzas

Preheat the oven to 250°C/480°F/gas mark 9 or as high as it will go. Place a pizza stone or an upside-down baking tray in the oven to heat up too. Get all your ingredients and equipment ready, including taking the dough out of the fridge 1 hour before you're ready to cook.

While the oven is heating up, place the cream in a mixing bowl and whisk until soft peaks form.

Roll out the dough as per the instructions on page 25 (the chocolate dough is too stiff to stretch by hand). Prick the dough all over with the tines of a fork so that it doesn't puff up too much in the oven, since it's being baked on its own without any toppings.

Slide the pizza off the peel or board onto the pizza stone or upside-down baking tray in the hot oven. Cook for about 5 minutes, until the dough is cooked through.

Take the pizza out of the oven and push it down if it has puffed up too much. Don't worry if the dough cracks a little when you do this, as it will get covered up with the toppings. Transfer to a wire cooling rack and allow to cool for at least 5 minutes because the whipped cream will melt if the base is too hot.

Dollop over the whipped cream and spread it evenly over the cooled base using the back of a spoon or a palette knife, leaving a 2.5 cm (1 in) border clear around the edges for the crust. Scatter the sliced bananas evenly across the top and drizzle with the toffee sauce, then grate over the chocolate by running a vegetable peeler along the long edge of the bar. Use a long chef's knife rather than a pizza cutter to cut into slices.

INDEX

ACKNOWLEDGMENTS

I would like to thank all the people who have given me so much support and encouragement over the years. This book has been a wonderful experience of working with great people.

My mother-in-law, Darina Allen, once suggested that I write a book on butchery, but something never felt quite right about it. One day I bumped into her at the Ballymaloe Café and she told me that she'd been talking to somebody who thought it would be a good idea for me to write a pizza book, and her name was Kristin Jensen. I rang Kristin and left a message. A few days later I was driving through the Black Forest in Germany with my mother when the phone rang and Kristin and I had our first conversation about the book. She asked me how many different pizzas I had done over the years. I thought for a moment and did some quick calculations in my head. 'About 200?' I said. 'Why don't we whittle it down to the 50 best pizzas?' she replied. And that was it – that's how this book basically came about. It's amazing what thought and action combined can create.

Thanks to Patrick Tracy and Lucy Pierce for their advice; to Tim and Darina for always giving your support; and to Emily, Zaiah and Betsy. Thank you to my brothers- and sisters-in-law, especially Rachel, for all your help.

To all the Saturday Pizzas staff, Katy McCarthy, Niamh McCarthy, Dylan Paul, Rowen Doyle, Rachel Flemming and Jack Penruddock – you guys have no idea how happy it makes me to have you on the team. A big thank you as well to all the regular Saturday Pizzas customers.

Thank you to all the staff at the Ballymaloe Cookery School and to Toby Allen for letting me share his office. Thank you as well to Rupert Hugh-Jones for high-quality inspiration.

Thanks to all the team at Ryland Peters & Small and to Sharon Bowers from Miller Bowers Griffin Literary Management.

And thank you to Mama, Papa, Ingo, Edgar, Brigitte and Gerda für eine wunderbare Kindheit.

Philip Dennhardt

Author(s): Stephen Haber
Author(s): Armando Razo
Author(s): Noel Maurer
Editor(s):

The Politics of Property Rights:
  Political Instability, Credible
  Commitments, and Economic Growth in
  Mexico, 1876-1929

2003

Hardback   0-521-82067-7 $75.00

For more information, please e-mail publicity@cup.org
or call 212-924-3900 x310.
We would appreciate three copies of the review. – Publicity Department